PESHTIGO

BY

GEORGE BAUER

Vabella Publishing
P.O. Box 1052
Carrollton, Georgia 30112
www.vabella.com

©Copyright 2017 by George Bauer

All rights reserved. The material contained herein is the property of George J. Bauer and may not be used, copied, or reproduced without the express written consent of the author.

Manufactured in the United States of America

13-digit ISBN 978-1-942766-40-7

Library of Congress Control Number 2017903853

10 9 8 7 6 5 4 3 2 1

For Susan and Lisa

Also by George Bauer:

The Seasoned Traveler: A Guide for Baby Boomers and Beyond
(companion book to Public Television travel program)

The End of Paradise
(Novel)

Acknowledgments:

The author wishes to note the contemporary and historical accounts of several authors, as well as information from the U.S. Government and other sources, which provided the background for this historical novel.

Among them:

Paul Metcalf, **"Firebird"** (Granary Books/Chax Press, 1987);

Reverend Peter Pernin, **"The Great Peshtigo Fire: An Eyewitness Account"** (The State Historical Society of Wisconsin, 1999);

Stephen J. Pyne, **"Fire in America: A Cultural History of Wildland and Rural Fire"** (Princeton University Press, 1982);

Alfred L. Sewell, **"The Great Calamity"** (Alfred L. Sewell, 1872);

William F. Steuber, Jr. **"The Landlooker"** (Bobbs-Merrill, 1957);

Franklin Tilton, **"Sketch of the Great Fires in Wisconsin at Peshtigo"** (Robinson Kustermann Publishers, 1871);

Robert W. Wells, **"Fire at Peshtigo"** (Prentice-Hall, 1968);

The National Interagency Fire Center, Boise, Idaho.

Foreword

The enduring drought that engulfed the Western regions of North America brought tinder-dry conditions, arid fields and farmlands, withered crops, and other related misery. Only heavy rain and snow in early 2017 ameliorated conditions.

But as 2017 dragged on, drought conditions returned to California and the American West. Hot weather and a lack of rainfall again dried fields and forests. By early October, 2017, the Golden State became a tinder-box once more. A series of wildfires broke out, fanned by ferocious winds that pushed the blazes across acre-after-acre of real estate, destroying thousands of homes and businesses in the process.

The inferno killed more than 40 people and California officials said it was the largest loss of life to wildfires in the state's history.

In early May of 2016, a massive wildfire, stoked by high winds, laid waste to a forested area near Fort McMurray, Alberta, Canada. It forced some 88,000 people to flee for their lives and damaged or destroyed 2,400 structures in the heart of Canada's oil sands region. Local officials said strong winds, high temperatures, and low humidity created the explosive conditions that led to the blazes.

It was merely the latest chapter in a seemingly-unending series of brushfires that have taken a toll on real estate in Canada and the United States.

The U.S. Forest Service noted that the 2015 wildfire season set a record, charring more than ten million acres of land across the country. More than half the acreage was burned in fires across Alaska, which suffered from historically low mountain snowpack and dry conditions that were fueled by a freak lightning storm. Washington, Oregon, California and other Western states also bore the brunt of blazes.

The wildfire danger plagued the West for years. Perhaps the most searing and tragic event in the 2013 fire season was the death of 19 firefighters on a ridge engulfed in flames near Yarnell, Arizona. The Granite Mountain Hotshot team was based in nearby Prescott and died in the Yarnell Hill firestorm on June 30.

According to the National Fire Protection Association, it was the largest loss of firefighters in a brushfire in 80 years, surpassed only by the 1933 Griffith Park blaze in California in which 29 firefighters perished and the deadly 1910 Devil's Broom fire in Idaho which killed 86 firemen.

The Yarnell tragedy represented the most fire crewmembers killed in the U.S. in a single event since September 11, 2001. On that fateful day, 341 firefighters and two paramedics were killed when New York's World Trade Center towers were struck by airliners and later collapsed.

Massive, blow-torch-like fires are part of American history. In 1910, a firestorm of Biblical proportions raged across the states of Washington, Idaho, and Montana, which included those firefighter deaths in Devil's Broom, Idaho. The Big Blowup burned for just two days, August twentieth and twenty-first, 1910, but it consumed three million acres in the Bitterroot Mountains (an area also devastated during the 2000 fire season). Entire towns were reduced to ashes. Thick smoke drifted in massive clouds, darkening the sky in northern states. In Watertown, New York, street lights remained on all day because of the murky darkness. The Big Blowup so frightened the entire nation that Congress decided for the first time in U.S. history to spend federal tax dollars fighting forest fires. The government ordered that all reported blazes must be extinguished by the next morning. Experts say such actions were ironic and may have contributed to the firestorms of later years. By combating blazes aggressively, the government prevented wildfires from performing a vital natural function: reducing vegetation that can fuel bigger blazes during protracted dry spells.

But two of the worst fires in U.S. history occurred the same day.

On October 8, 1871, a blaze broke out on the South Side of Chicago.

Tradition has it that a cow kicked over a kerosene lamp in a barn on South Dekoven Street, which ignited the straw-filled stable. The fire spread quickly through the city, fanned by high velocity winds.

The resulting blaze, dubbed by Chicago newspapers "The Great Calamity", burned for four and a half miles, consuming 18,000 buildings, three railroad depots, and seven bridges, for a total of $200 million in property damage, quite significant in those times.

Three hundred Chicagoans were killed. The Great Chicago Fire has become a significant event in United States history, understood by most school children.

As that blaze was destroying 2,400 acres in Chicago, a lesser-known conflagration 256 miles north of the Windy City charred 3,780,000 acres of tinder-dry timberland in Northern Wisconsin and the adjacent Upper Peninsula of Michigan. As many as 1,800 people died on both sides of the Green Bay in Wisconsin and 200 more perished in Michigan, seven times the toll in Chicago. Although several towns were affected, this series of blazes became known as the Peshtigo fire, the largest town in the region at the time.

One historian called the Peshtigo inferno "the worst tragedy of its kind ever recorded in North America".

The Peshtigo inferno was followed a decade later by a one-million-acre wildfire in September, 1881, in Michigan, which claimed one hundred, sixty-nine lives. Three Septembers later, Wisconsin was struck again by fires that charred millions of acres. That same month a blaze in Hinckley, Minnesota, destroyed a million acres of land and killed more than four hundred people. Major forest fires have broken out on a regular basis from then until now. Americans have learned to fear hurricanes, tornadoes, earthquakes, and floods. But wildfires have also been a devastating, and deadly, component of life in rural America.

What follows is the story of the drought of 1871 which created and spawned both the fire in Chicago and the cataclysm in Peshtigo.

It focuses on Northern Wisconsin, which was an area of several small towns and several more small farms in the surrounding countryside. Populating both were families, often large by today's standards. It was not uncommon for married couples to have four, six, even eight children. It often meant more hands to help with the hard work that went with backwoods living.

This book is based on actual accounts of the fires but it is an historical novel. The names of communities are authentic, as are the family names of many residents. *Peshtigo* profiles about a dozen families who lived during the time. The region's residents were largely private people, so their daily activities and even their children's names are uncertain or unknown. In this case, the author has taken literary license in naming them and describing their daily routine.

Some of these families survived the flames on October 8th, while others encountered horrible deaths.

As the story of the actual fire unfolds, countless others will be mentioned. They were among the thousands who suffered on that infamous day. While the people are important, it is the fires that are of foremost importance in this book, which is written to help readers understand the events that led to the deadliest fire in our country's history. It is also a tribute to the men, women, children, and animals who lived and died during the firestorm.

More Americans should know about the Great Peshtigo Fire, for it has burnished its place in the nation's history.

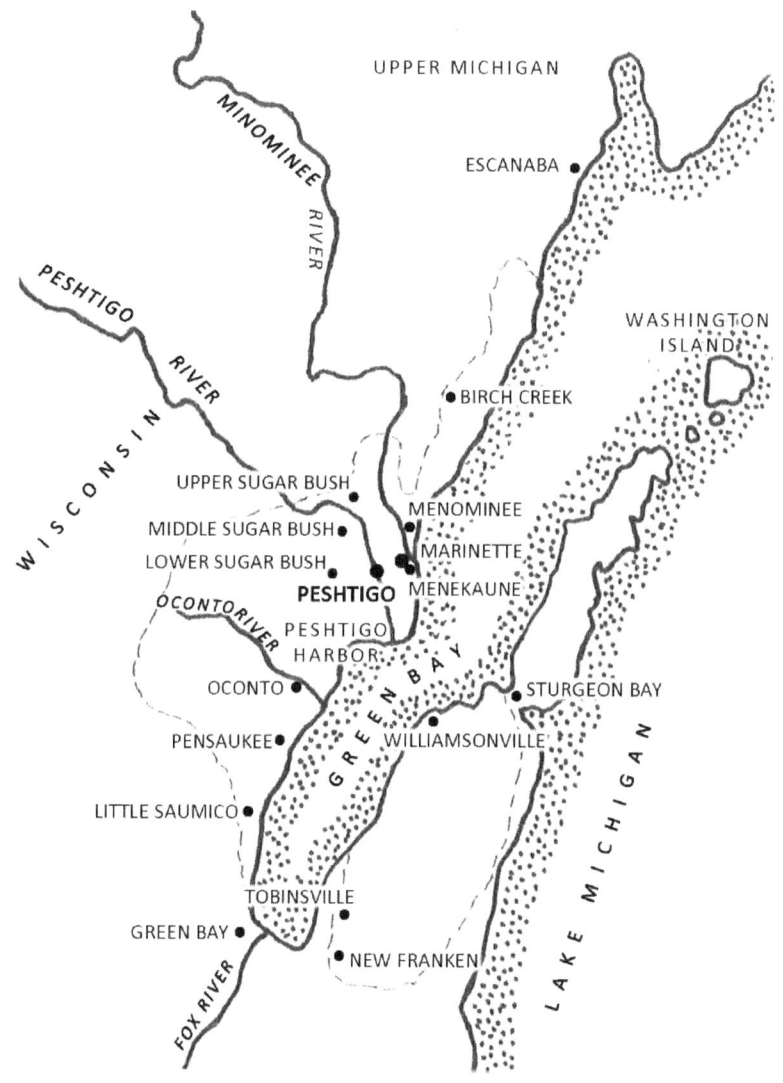

Prologue

Near the source of the Oconto River, perhaps fifty miles northwest of Green Bay, Wisconsin, the heat became intense, unusual for early autumn. It drifted upward from the parched pine-forested land, similar to a mushroom cloud from an atomic bomb blast many decades later, and then collided with the upper-level air, producing lightning.

Massive bolts of electricity darted across the crystal-clear late-September sky.

This happened not once but scores of times. There were no accompanying claps of thunder following the lightning shower. And there was no moisture in the heavens for hundreds of miles, so there were not the slightest hints of rain clouds gathering. It was just a dangerous nighttime fireworks display deep in the forests of the Upper Midwest.

Given the frequency and ferocity of these celestial fire-rods, some lightning bolts inevitably reached from deep into the night sky all the way down to the desiccated earth below.

The power of the strikes caused violent explosions as the electrical shocks blew trees apart sending bark, limbs, and leaves hurtling through the tepid air. Sparks flew hundreds of feet, falling on drought-dried trees, withered leaves, and dead underbrush, igniting them.

As trees toppled and other lightning strikes fomented further explosions, the flames, heat, and haze terrorized forest creatures on and under the ground, those who lived in trees, and the birds which normally flew above it all.

Animals great and small screeched and cried and ran for safety, not really knowing where to run or hide. Several were killed as the lightning toppled trees. Birds were killed as they attempted to escape the burning forest, only to fly into flames and smoke, which asphyxiated them. Other animals were trapped and burned to death.

The death and destruction were muted, however, because these outbreaks of fire in the first days of autumn, 1871, were far from civilization. No humans were aware of the catastrophe.

Peshtigo

But with the expanding dry conditions, the inferno spread, unheralded and unchecked by rain, streams, or human intervention. Vast clouds of smoke and ash billowed aloft, carried eastward by the prevailing winds that blew steadily that season.

Those winds sent the smoke and fire ever closer to the small but growing communities of Northern Wisconsin, the prosperous lumber towns of this once-green section of the state.

And what the residents of the region did not know was that larger and more devastating fires were not far away.

Chapter 1

September 22, 1871.

A loud shriek pierced the stillness and darkness surrounding the young girl's bed. The outburst gave way to crying, which awakened her brothers and sisters sleeping nearby, but they did not move. The girl's mother came running from another room.

"There, there, my child. What is it?" she inquired.

"Mama, the fire had come," the girl replied. "The house was on fire. I was trapped and couldn't get out!" She whimpered into her mother's bosom as the woman cradled and hugged her frightened daughter.

"It's all right, baby. We will not let the fire hurt us. God will protect us all."

Young Colleen Towsley's nocturnal outburst may not have been unique in Northern Wisconsin. For thousands of people in many small towns, the threat of fire was omnipresent.

A smoky smell permeated the autumn air after a long, dry summer. Indeed, Wisconsin had been suffering through a drought for the entire year. The last heavy rain had fallen on the eighth of July but the ground was already so parched, it drank in the water like a human dying of thirst. There had been a sprinkle or two in early September but it had no effect on the widespread drought that had Wisconsin and the Upper Peninsula of Michigan in its unending grip. Even swamps had dried up.

The unusual and unwelcome weather had begun months earlier and had been a constant source of discussion in the half-dozen counties that clung to Wisconsin's Green Bay. Winter snowfall from 1870 and early 1871 had been negligible, a rarity in a region renowned for harsh winters of low temperatures and heaping snow. But rather than providing a cause for celebration, the mild winter became a cause of serious concern among the residents and business-leaders in the tinder-dry region.

Northern Wisconsin and adjacent Michigan were areas of abundance, brimming with millions of acres of timber, ripe and ready for harvesting. "A limitless sea of pine" was the description of one local businessman for this vast stretch of virgin forest, although other tree varieties were also plentiful.

And with the youthful nation growing and expanding, the demand for wood and wood products was increasing. Forestry had become a leading industry in Wisconsin as it celebrated its twenty-third year of statehood, the thirtieth admitted to the Union.

All across the normally-green, tree-laden area, near towns called Peshtigo and Oconto and Sugar Bush and Williamsonville, workers sawed trees deep in the woods. Horses and oxen dragged the logs to mills in nearby communities, where they were reduced to wood planks or boards, or refined further into useful products. Most of these products were then sent by ship to other parts of the country while some wood would be transported by railroad from Northern Wisconsin, south to Milwaukee and Chicago.

But the dry winter, spring, and summer had interfered with the normal wood-harvesting routine. The absence of winter snow and spring rain meant the sea of pines was more like a dry bed and a fire hazard. The drought had been so long and so deep that by late summer fires began breaking out in the woods.

Colleen Towsley lived on a farm in Oconto, the youngest of four Towsley children. Her blue eyes, honey-brown hair, and dimples led her father to call her "my adorable daughter". C.R. Towsley grew corn on twenty acres of flat, stone-studded but nutrient-rich Wisconsin crop land. The family farm also raised sheep for wool, kept two large horses to help plow the fields and pull the family wagon, and had a pair of cows which provided enough milk for the family's dairy needs.

C.R. Towsley was an ox of a man, tall and beefy with a shock of auburn hair atop his large head and across his face in the form of a full beard. His wife Annabelle had borne him an equal number of male and female offspring. While she appeared small and frail Annabelle was strong-willed and strong of spirit. She wore her dark hair pulled tightly into a bun at the back of her small head. She worked as hard as her husband doing farm chores, then cleaning the house, cooking the meals, and caring for the children. She once told her husband that while he worked hard from sunrise to dark, her work never ended.

Jonathan was the eldest Towsley child and, at sixteen, was his father's right-hand man, both in running the farm and milking the cows each day. Tall and thin, he was considered handsome by the local girls his age but he had little time for socializing. Mayme, at fourteen, was her mother's right-hand woman, helping with the cooking, baking, butter-churning, and putting up preserves and pickles. Her father often said Mayme's fair-skinned beauty and flowing brown hair worried him because of the crazed young suitors who might swarm the farm seeking her attention and her affection.

Eleven-year-old Bradford Towsley took after his father in many ways, the most prominent of which was his full head of red hair. His responsibilities included tending the horses, cows, and sheep as well as the family dogs. And when his father or big brother required assistance, Brad was called upon to help. Brad had a secret passion: he loved to read and spent as much spare time as he could with his face buried in a book.

Because Colleen was just eight, her tasks were lighter and included setting the table for meals and cleaning up afterwards. She also tended the vegetable garden each summer with her mother.

It was a hard life but the Towsley family were considered successful and comfortable. The corn crop generally paid the bills. The sale of wool covered luxuries. The abundant woodlands provided ample fuel to heat the house during the long winters. The Towsleys said their prosperity was a measure of God's goodness. The family members were devout Roman Catholics who attended Sunday Mass at the still-unfinished church in Peshtigo. In fact, C.R. was one of the parishioners volunteering his labor to complete the construction. He was giving back for all he'd received. The Towsleys had many friends in the community and were respected by many others.

But the family's comfort and well-being had been hindered lately by the protracted drought conditions. The corn fields wilted, stalks were stunted and C.R. Towsley worried he would have no corn to sell in 1871 and would be forced to dip into the family's savings to get through the year. Annabelle had another concern. The lack of rain meant the well water was depleting, slowly but steadily. She also fretted about the health of both the children and the animals, subjected to ever-more-frequent clouds of smoke as more wildfires broke out off in the woods.

On some days the air was thick with choking smoke. Mrs. Towsley told her husband it was not good for the children to be inhaling such foul air. He agreed but they both knew there was nothing that could be done to alleviate the condition until steady rains doused the area.

The Towsleys lived west of the Green Bay near the town of Oconto, seat of Oconto County, located along the Oconto River, which drained into the Bay. Oconto was ten miles north of the city of Green Bay, the largest community in Northern Wisconsin, and seven miles southwest of Peshtigo, the most prominent town in the region. By 1871, Oconto County boasted fourteen thousand residents, most of whom made their living by farming or forestry.

Now, deep into this October night as Colleen Towsley's mother comforted her and tried to diminish the fire danger, she was unaware of some wind-whipped fires that had increased in size between Oconto and Green Bay, one of which came within a few miles of the larger city. Only minor casualties were reported. But another fire was more deadly. An Indian man and team of horses burned to death when a wildfire broke out north of Oconto surrounding the man's barn and reducing it to ash before either the man or his beasts could escape. The fire might have been far worse but the wind died down abruptly and the fire burned itself out before reaching the end of the victim's property.

When C.R. Towsley read his local newspaper the night before, he came upon an account of a smoky siege in the western woods:

"The whole air is filled with a dense, suffocating smoke, almost obscuring the vision, over a tract hundreds of square miles. The sun shone through the smoke with a red, angry glare. The heavens at night would be illuminated on every side with the holocaust of fire."

Disaster seemed imminent, unless the unexpected occurred miraculously. The region needed rain and a calming of the winds.

The morning after Colleen's outburst, C.R. Towsley entered the house following a frustrating tour of his corn fields. He kissed his wife on the cheek.

"The crop does not look good," he announced in a low voice, unwilling to provoke additional anxiety among the children. "I tasted an ear of corn and it has a thick, smoky taste. I cannot imagine anyone buying it and I doubt cattle or hogs would eat it either." He went to the kitchen sink and scooped some well-water from a bucket. He took one long drink, then a second.

"My throat is parched and sore from breathing the smoke," C.R. said. "My God, I wish it would rain."

Towsley turned to his wife of two decades, the woman he loved and cherished, who had borne his children, endured the bad years on the farm, and celebrated the good seasons along with him.

"I am worried, Annie," he said. "The ground is so dry that any spark will ignite a fire and it will move so quickly we may not be able to react."

He waited just a few seconds.

"And there is one more thing. I talked with Joshua Clements today at his farm. His wife said the elders of the Menominee Tribe believe it has never been so dry at this time of year. The tribe blames the lumbermen and mill owners for all this, saying they are destroying the natural forests, so they are being punished for their actions."

*   *   *

Joshua Clements sat on the front porch of his small wooden cabin, just a few miles from the Towsley farm. As he awaited his supper, Clements was aware of two distinctive smells–the rabbit stew simmering in the kitchen fireplace, and the omnipresent odor of burning grass, leaves, and trees.

J.G. Clements, the name he used on official documents, had lived in Oconto just five years. He was twenty-eight years of age but seemed older and wiser. Clements had decided to leave his family in Milwaukee back in 1866 to strike out on his own and perhaps to strike it rich in forestry or agriculture.

With the money he had saved over the years and with some financial aid from his parents, he moved to Northern Wisconsin, bought five acres of land, built a tiny house and an even smaller barn.

He was tall and thin, with dark hair and eyes to match, not overly attractive, and very shy. But the decision to face his future on his own had raised his level of self-confidence. Times were tough at first and Joshua engaged in subsistence farming, planting vegetables in a garden plot and keeping two chickens, a cow, and four sheep. His limited income came from the lambs' wool and the trees he allowed area lumbermen to chop in the wooded corner of his small spread.

Then Joshua had met a charming young girl, a member of the Menominee Indian Tribe. Her name was Felice and she often came to the village of Oconto to sell leather goods. She was six years younger than he. When the young woman journeyed into town, on the second Saturday of each month, Joshua always managed to be there too and he never failed to engage her in conversation, sometimes even purchasing some of her leather wares. He was mesmerized by her, her olive-skinned good looks, coy shyness, her captivating smile. He was also intrigued by her background as a member of a Native American tribe.

After several months, he knew he was in love with the petite young woman with the flowing black hair. On one of her visits to town, in a moment of spontaneous exuberance, J.G. Clements asked Felice to marry him. She was, at first, shocked by his overture. Her family was troubled with the idea of the proposed union, wishing to maintain Menominee lineage unfettered by the genes of a Caucasian from Southern Wisconsin.

Yet, even though her father and mother protested the arrangement, Felice found herself feeling more deeply for Joshua and arguing that she should be allowed to marry the man she loved, Menominee or white. After some time, her family consented reluctantly to the marriage but required that two ceremonies be held, a tribal marriage in Menominee territory and a ceremony of Joshua's choosing.

When Felice became Mrs. J.G. Clements, she appeared to blossom, away from the confines and strictures of her Indian family and she brought order to the chaos of Joshua's life and home. Felice plotted and planted a large and expansive garden, then put up fruits and vegetables for winter consumption. She assisted her husband in minding the animals. And she was the perfect wife, companion, friend, and lover. Joshua was often stunned by the poise and maturity she demonstrated for a woman so young.

Joshua Clements allowed local lumber barons to harvest just a handful of trees per year in the most heavily-forested sector of his acreage but the income was helpful to the newlyweds. Each year when the lumberjacks, who were called shanty boys, vacated the Clements property after their cutting, they left behind cold hard cash and warm piles of wood chips and sawdust. In most years, this was a neutral remnant. The wood fragments would be disbursed by the wind and moistened by rain and snow. But as the drought of 1871 worsened, the desiccated wood bits on the parched earth increased the risk that fires might spread quickly through the Clements land, perhaps endangering the home and barn.

Despite the added income, Felice did not like the lumberjacks or their wealthy employers. This distrust was inculcated by her family and other members of the tribe, who rued the steady influx of people into the area around the Green Bay. The Indians resented the taking of the land by the whites, the construction of new towns and the railroad, not to mention the denuding of the rich forests. The tribe blamed the whites for the current meteorological setback. The logging practices, they said, had angered the Great Spirit who was now punishing them for destroying nature. And they predicted there would be an even more severe penalty to pay.

So Felice and Joshua prepared for the worst and took steps to protect their property from ruin. They dug a perimeter-ditch around the cabin and barn to prevent fire from storming across the fields and the garden--incinerating the buildings and the wood fencing used to corral the animals. Joshua purchased half a dozen barrels from the local wood factory. He placed them strategically around the house and filled them with water, to douse fires that might pose a threat. They turned over great swathes of land, exposing the dirt, to slow or stop any fire that might rush from their wooded land toward the house. And they invoked the Great Spirit to protect them from whatever flames and smoke might come their way.

While Joshua remained on edge, ever-worried that fire would eventually strike, Felice maintained a silent, stoic optimism. She felt certain she and her husband could survive any blazes. The power of the Great Spirit gave her comfort and confidence.

Chapter 2

October 1, 1871.

Forest fires ringed the town of Peshtigo, far from populated areas but the effects were already noticeable. They smoldered across an area about one hundred miles long, seventy miles wide. Occasionally a fire was whipped into a furious frenzy, as the wind fanned in one direction, then another. The winds were a constant.

In the center of town the hymn-singing was loud and long, leaking through the walls of the Congregational Church. This house of God was crammed with worshipers. They had come to pray for deliverance from the blazes, asking that the fires burn themselves out or bypass Peshtigo altogether. And there was another urgent request.

"Please God!" they implored the Almighty, "make it rain."

On a typical Sunday, a respectable number of residents would enter the church for Sunday services. But with a heightened threat of impending doom, attendance had been swelling during the Sundays of September and it had become a crush on this first Lord's Day of October. The Congregational Church was the only religious edifice in the town.

The Roman Catholic community was building its own church but it was still unfinished. Episcopalians met in the town's Good Templars Hall. The Evangelical Lutheran Church met in a local hall.

As the people of Peshtigo prayed and sang, they drew acrid smoke into their lungs, coughing as they worshiped. There was a community-wide fear developing that future growth and prosperity were threatened even though Peshtigo was on the verge of becoming a boom town and lumber was at the heart of it.

Thirty-five years earlier, in 1836, a man called David Jones had come to Northern Wisconsin to cash in on the endless forests. He built a small mill near the river to allow transport of logs and finished products to markets farther south. Within a few years, Jones laid out a street grid and sold lots for homes. As the town took shape, other eventual lumber kingpins began arriving. They bought vast quantities of timberland from the government for just a dollar and a quarter per acre.

Isaac Stephenson was another pioneer. He first set foot in the town in 1845 and ultimately became one of Peshtigo's elders and scions, wielding wealth and power. Another local lumber leader, Cadwalladcr Washburn, parlayed his fame and fortune to the top seat of state government. He became Governor of Wisconsin.

The men who made the initial investments were followed by hundreds of other men, and fewer women, who had no money to invest but who wanted to work in the burgeoning new industry, harvesting all those forests. Sixty lumber camps eventually sprang up, operating at full throttle each winter, the time when trees were felled. The lumberjacks worked long and hard but when the work-week ended, they collected fat paychecks and herded to places quite eager to take their earnings.

Peshtigo, a Chippewa expression meaning "river of the wild goose", saw its population surge to more than two thousand. It boasted fourteen saloons on both sides of the Peshtigo River, which sliced the community in half. Near the bars stood other diversions, including several brothels which did extensive flesh-trade from Friday until Sunday.

To fulfill citizens' other needs, several shops sprouted along the town's main thoroughfare, Oconto Street. Kelsey and Vierke's Pharmacy was co-owned by Peshtigo's only physician, J.F. Kelsey. The dry goods and grocery store down the street was the property of F.J. Bartels. Nearby was the Peshtigo Hardware store. George Robinson opened a butcher shop. And, as wealth increased, luxury items appeared. J.F. Jaques moved to town and sold pianos, organs, and melodeons. And a shop from Marinette, Wisconsin, opened a Peshtigo branch. Harter and Horvath sold clothing, lace, and embroidery.

There were several hotels in the community. The Jacobs, the Peshtigo, the Forest House, and the Hotel de France were used for visitors to town or those who had just moved in but had yet to find permanent accommodations. All the business people were enthusiastic about the completion of a railroad line to their backwoods community. The Chicago and Northwestern Railroad

Peshtigo

was building the link. It would haul logs and wood products south, while bringing new residents and workers north to Peshtigo.

The town's most prominent corporate citizen was the Peshtigo Company, which boasted a sawmill, a related factory to make wood products, and offices which served as the center of operations for both the timber operation and a cranberry-growing business, another new Wisconsin product. The company planned to cultivate a thousand acres of bog-land, one of the town's earliest attempts at corporate diversification.

As more people moved in, homes were built on the plots platted by David Jones nearly a half-century earlier. Given the vast natural wealth surrounding the town, the houses were made of logs or boards and had wooden shingles on their roofs. The streets out front were paved with split logs and covered with brush. Sidewalks were actually boardwalks, which people appreciated during rainy, snowy, or muddy periods. Bridges connecting the eastern and western sides of town were built of planks, supported by wooden timbers.

And from the Peshtigo Company mill, piles of sawdust and wood shavings were dumped across the community. In most years, wind and weather dispersed or diminished much of the mess. But when the mountains of slashings, as they were called, became too high workers removed them as a safety precaution. Workers shoveled the wood chips into wagons and hauled them several miles before dumping the waste into the waters of Green Bay.

Peshtigo's population jumped to fourteen-thousand when the drought began and as it worsened, residents worried more. They expressed growing alarm that there had been no major snowfalls in the winter of 1870-'71 and almost no rain since winter ended. Their concerns led them to take concrete precautions but also to flood churches to beg for salvation.

A week earlier, Peshtigo had been virtually cut off from Green Bay and Oconto as gusts stoked fires in the woods south of town. Residents gathered in the center of Peshtigo and discussed how they would battle any blazes which might reach their community. Water barrels were refilled and volunteer firefighters of all ages were put on alert.

On Sunday, September 24th, the fire-watch was interrupted briefly as men, women and children snaked their way to their respective houses of worship.

But after folks had consumed Sunday dinner, the breeze resumed, blowing from the northwest. Word went out that another firestorm was building and moving ominously closer. Residents had been so concerned about the fires to the south, from Oconto and Green Bay that they had all but missed this new threat coming from the other direction.

The fire approached Peshtigo. Some families on the northern edge of town began evacuating their homes. They crossed the river for protection. Firemen rushed to the northern part of the community and formed long lines of bucket brigades near the likely path of the fire. As the wind blew it closer, the teams began a systematic attempt to douse the advancing flames. And with continuous backbreaking work, the water-carriers managed to prevent the blaze from getting out of control.

As darkness fell, the wind subsided once again. The fire lost its sustenance and died out. This one was finished. This neighborhood was saved.

Later that night, relieved residents re-crossed the river and returned to their now-spared dwellings. Peshtigo was safe for another day but the weary firefighters knew conditions could change at any time.

The Peshtigo Company announced it was closing its factory for the day so those who fought the Sunday fire could rest.

David Maxon was among those with the day off. He and his family had lived in Wisconsin for some five years, arriving after a harrowing trip from New England. David and his pregnant wife Priscilla had trudged into town with three young children in tow. They had made the dangerous journey by wagon from Manchester, New Hampshire, where David worked in a textile mill along the Merrimack River, not knowing from day-to-day whether Priscilla might have to stop to give birth.

Both David and Priscilla were born and raised in that old New England mill-town, living just a few blocks apart. The two attended the same schools and the friendship of classmates eventually blossomed into abiding affection, love and eventually marriage.

Peshtigo

Of average height, with close-cropped brown hair and a ready smile, David Maxon elected to stay in his hometown and work for a local textile producer when he finished his schooling. Petite, dark-haired, fair-skinned, and friendly, Priscilla Maxon was glad her husband had chosen work in Manchester and decided against moving to northern New Hampshire's forests, where hundreds of men spent long hours sawing logs for large paper mills. David did well in his job and made a good living.

The Maxons found a small house about half a mile from the Manchester mill. It was a pleasant walk to and from work for David and for Priscilla, a walk of half that distance took her to the local market and other shops. Life was good, so good that David was spared having to fight for Northern troops in the Civil War. His work at the mill was considered so crucial to the Union cause that he never left the Granite State during the dismal confrontation between the North and the South.

The War was profitable for the textile mill and for Manchester. Business boomed. But when the War Between the States finally ended and the reunified nation began to rebuild, many mill owners discovered cheaper land, cheaper labor, and lower production costs in what had been the Confederacy. The owners of David Maxon's factory did the arithmetic and opted to end operations in New England and relocate to the New South.

David and Priscilla were crushed. Their options were few: move to the South with the mill owners and work for lower wages, stay in New Hampshire and seek alternative work just as jobs were becoming scarce, or consider other opportunities elsewhere. The Maxons came to the painful conclusion that the last option was probably the most appropriate. He had read about prospects at the lumber mills and wood factories in the growing towns of Northern Wisconsin and Michigan's Upper Peninsula. With few other options, David Maxon concluded that opportunity was knocking in the Midwest, so he purchased a covered wagon and two large horses and packed the family belongings into the wagon.

Along with their children, Adam, Mary and Caleb, the Maxons set off for new horizons on the western frontier. With the few hundred dollars he had saved over the years, David knew the family could survive for several weeks until he found employment.

It was early May. The trek through the seven states took two months. In July 1866, the Maxons rolled into Peshtigo. Although it was smaller, the town looked similar to the Manchester they had left behind. A river ran through it, there were mills and factories, and a growing number of shops and hotels. The family took two rooms at a boarding house, one for the adults and the other for the children. Priscilla decided Adam, Mary and Caleb were young enough to share not only a room but also a bed. Things would improve, she knew, once David found work and they located a new home.

David didn't waste a day and went immediately in search of work. His first stop was the Peshtigo Company mill and woodworking plant. He succeeded on his second inquiry and was offered a job at the factory.

The Peshtigo Company crafted many of the logs harvested in the Wisconsin woods. Among the items it produced were wooden shingles, broom handles, clothes pins, barrel heads, pails and wooden tubs.

David Maxon was hired to work on the assembly line that turned out broom handles and clothes pegs. He earned about three-quarters of what he had made in New Hampshire but he discovered that the cost of living was lower in Wisconsin. So, with his new wage and what remained of his savings, David felt justified with his decision to uproot his young family and bring them halfway across the continent to the town of Peshtigo.

Eventually David was able to put a deposit on a small parcel of land near the west bank of the Peshtigo River. He contacted a local builder and agreed to work with him in constructing a new home for the family because David wanted to be settled in before winter. As the construction began, David Maxon worked extra hours and received bonuses for his hard work. He looked forward that year to Christmas, knowing he could afford a new home and gifts for his wife and children.

On September 24th, 1871, David Maxon was one of the many volunteers fighting the fire that threatened to encroach on the community but which was smothered by the bucket brigade's determination.

"I am protecting the town where I live and work," Maxon said, "and I'm protecting my family and property too."

Peshtigo

Since their arrival in Peshtigo, the Maxon family had increased by two. Adam, the eldest, had just turned twelve. He was skinny and freckle-faced, with light brown hair. His parents treated him as a third adult. Adam had helped his father with fire precautions and even helped on the bucket lines on the night of the fire, until he became too fatigued to continue.

Daughter Mary was now nine. David Maxon was proud of his first daughter. "The spittin' image of her beautiful mother," he used to say.

Eight-year-old Caleb was a happy-go-lucky, energetic youngster who seemed to wear out other family members with his non-stop chatter and constant motion.

Soon after their arrival in Peshtigo, Priscilla gave birth to a second daughter, Tess. Now five-years-old, Tess was a plain child, frail, and often sickly. Her parents assumed it was related to the stress that Priscilla endured during the long trip from the East. They worried about the child's health for years but especially over the last several weeks as heavy smoke in the air made breathing difficult for everyone.

The newest family-member was Zachary who, at age three, was fair-haired and fair-skinned, looking very much like his mother.

The Maxons had a three-bedroom clapboard house in Peshtigo. Wooden shingles adorned the roof, products of the Peshtigo Company woodenware factory. There was nearly an acre of land surrounding the house, home to the horses and the wagon that brought the Maxons from New England to their new life.

On the morning after the rest-day mandated by officials of the Company, David Maxon left home for work. He put in his normal ten-hour workday but when he returned home that evening, he found all was not well.

Priscilla did not greet him at the front door, as was her custom. She was, in fact, lying sick in the bed she shared with her husband. She was perspiring and very pale.

"What is it, my dear?" David Maxon inquired, when he came to the bedside.

"I think I have a fever", she feebly replied. "Adam went to get Dr. Kelsey, who was here earlier and .....", but she seemed to forget the thread of her sentence and abandoned any attempt to complete it.

"Did he give you medicine?" David asked. But before she could answer, his attention turned to a bottle of liquid on the bedside table. "There it is, let me have a look".

The label on the medicine explained that the contents were to be used as a fever reducer and calming agent.

J.F. Kelsey was Peshtigo's only physician. He was also co-owner of the town's drug store. Doc Kelsey saw patients in his office but more often tended to make house-calls to the sick. He carried two black bags. One contained his medical paraphernalia while a much larger satchel was filled with remedies, pills and potions - some that may have had medicinal merit and others that likely did little in combating illness or disease. One of those remedies sat on Priscilla Maxon's bedside table.

"Now you rest, Prissy, and I'll check in on you later," David told his wife. "Do you need anything now?"

"I just want to sleep," she responded and became quiet once more.

David withdrew quietly from the bedroom and walked towards the kitchen, where his two oldest children had taken on the task of preparing dinner. Adam and Mary were pan-frying some left-over chicken, boiling potatoes and carrots, and slicing some bread.

"Good work, children," David complimented them. "Is there anything I can do?"

They assured him that all was under control and that dinner would be ready in fifteen minutes. David Maxon left the kitchen and went out onto the back porch where he threw warm water on his face. He dried himself, combed his hair, and went to the parlor. As he sat awaiting his evening meal, he hoped the fire and smoke of recent days had not adversely affected his wife. And he uttered a silent prayer that Priscilla would soon recover.

Chapter 3

October 5, 1871.

By now, the fire danger in Northern Wisconsin was expanding exponentially. In deep forests on both sides of Green Bay, acre after acre of tree-covered land became fodder for the insatiable, wind-driven fires. The fire-band looked like a monstrous horse-shoe stretching around the southern end of the bay. To the east, residents of Door and Kewaunee counties reported numerous blazes of varying sizes. The towns of Williamsonville on the north and New Franken to the south were affected by fire, smoke, and haze. On the western side of Green Bay, new fires broke out near Marinette, some seven miles north of Peshtigo, and west of Oconto.

Traditionally, October was the most magnificent month in this northern clime. As daylight dwindled and the thermometer dropped, the crisp, cool conditions normally created a panorama of color. The leaves from millions of trees metamorphosed into brilliant hues and tints. Bright yellows and oranges, blazing scarlets, and golden rusts combined with the remnants of green to create a natural kaleidoscope that surpassed the work of any artist.

But the autumnal transformation required normal weather patterns. Trees and leaves needed moisture to remain healthy during the growing season, so that when the cold sapped their strength, the leaves would have enough vitality to produce the breathtaking leaves. But as the Fall of 1871 progressed, there was no symphony of color. Leaves were so desiccated they were unable to develop their normal brilliant colors. They had long-ago shriveled, hanging lifeless from their branches.

Among the trees that produced the bountiful colors in a good year were sugar maples that grew in abundance west of Peshtigo. And normally at this time of year, the maples would boast leaves of stunning crimson. Those who saw the maples were awed by their beauty.

Within the sugar maple forest, three small towns had been settled and they had become the most prosperous in the region. Lower Sugar Bush, Middle Sugar Bush, and Upper Sugar Bush were close-knit communities. Residents owned large tracts of land which generally yielded large profits. The farm families worked hard all week, played hard at parties or dances on Saturday evening, then rested on Sunday after attending church services.

Charles Lamb owned a 150-acre wheat farm in the northernmost Sugar Bush settlement. He was a tall, gaunt man, spare of speech and down-to-earth, who labored long in his fields and tended chickens which produced about fifty eggs each day. He sold them to the owner of the General Store in town.

His wife Nellie was the quintessential Irish lass. She had come to the United States with her family at the height of Ireland's infamous potato famine. The family had gone first to Chicago but when Nellie's father tired of urban living, he moved his wife and five children to Northern Wisconsin where he became a hard-working lumberman by day and a hard-drinking lumberman at night.

Nellie met Charles Lamb at a dance in Peshtigo. After two years of low-intensity courting, the shy Charles finally summoned the courage to seek her hand in marriage. She accepted and the wedding was held shortly thereafter. Nellie left her family and moved to Charles Lamb's farm.

That was ten years ago. As the couple celebrated its first anniversary, Nellie announced she was pregnant. Joseph Lamb entered the world eight years ago and, just as Nellie had become used to caring for her infant, she was again with child. Mary Lamb was born seven years ago. The couple's third child came two years after Mary, a boy called Carl.

The Lamb home was as impressive as the farming operation Charles commanded. The wood frame house had three large bedrooms and three rooms for family living. It was one of the few homes in the region with a separate dining room, furnished with an expensive mahogany dining table and eight matching chairs made by craftsmen in Pennsylvania.

Charles and Nellie had two vastly different personalities. She was outgoing, quick to smile, demonstrating an Irish playfulness and sense of humor. She was far more gregarious than he, both at home and with others. When the Lambs were together, Nellie was generally talking, Charles likely listening. And she had one other noticeable trait. Nellie made it obvious that her children were her life. She loved them deeply so she protected them and fawned over them, day-in and day-out.

For Charles, maintaining the health of his farm and business interests meant wealth for himself, his wife, and their children. He pursued that goal vigorously. But as the drought dragged on through 1871, Charles Lamb fretted about the safety and productivity of his wheat crop and the chickens. Small fires burned intermittently in the forests near his property. So far, at least, the winds had diverted them from the farm. Still, the fires created clouds of smoke, which spread over the Lamb land like a heavy winter blanket. It brought tears to Charles' eyes and a parched lump to his throat as he headed each day into the fields.

On this particular morning, visibility was reduced dramatically as Charles stood near his house. What troubled him was that he could not see the tree-line at the end of his plowed fields. He also noted a new and ominous threat– the distant fires sent burning embers aloft, which the winds blew for miles. They had the unsettling tendency of drifting down onto peoples' hair and clothing, as well as the tinder-dry fields and gardens. Charles himself watched as an ember ignited a clump of dry grass near his chicken coop. He ran to fetch a bucket of water nearby and doused the fire before any serious damage was done.

"Our whole world could soon go up in flames," Nellie Lamb said one evening at the mahogany dining table.

"Now, Ma, don't upset the children," her husband warned. "With any luck it will rain again soon." Nellie Lamb remained silent after her husband's gentle rebuke but she doubted his prediction. She had become increasingly worried as conditions deteriorated.

"Yes, my love," replied Nellie, "with God's help, even rains are possible."

* * *

In Middle Sugar Bush, Alfred Phillips and his wife Mildred were living their Golden Years. They owned three hundred acres, which had been extremely productive and rewarding over the years. Alfred was a grain farmer, rotating crops every few years to protect his soil from exhaustion. He simultaneously raised hogs and had about a hundred animals penned a great distance from the Phillips home. They were sent to Green Bay for slaughter, three or four at a time transported by wagon to the meat-packing district.

The Phillips family was considered wealthy, not in the league of the lumber barons, but Alfred was known around the area as a gentleman farmer because he hired several local men as farmhands. This left him time to engage in other endeavors; he was active in town government affairs and donated the funds to build and furnish the local schoolhouse. It was one of the most impressive buildings in the village. Mildred volunteered her time for other projects, spearheading a drive to create a lending library for the town. She and a few other socially-prominent neighbors succeeded in securing a room in the local bank building, collecting and buying books, and raising money to hire a part-time librarian.

The Phillips' marital union had produced a son, Alfred Junior, known as Fred to distinguish him from his father, who preferred to be addressed by his full name. The younger Phillips lived what could only be described as a charmed life, never needing to engage in farm work and not required to perform household chores. Fred had time to excel in his studies at the local school, which led him beyond the boundaries of Northern Wisconsin. Fred Phillips became one of the few local residents to move away from the area. He attended the relatively-young University of Wisconsin at Madison, which was chartered in 1848, then remained in the capital city to work for the state government. Fred visited his parents at Sugar Bush twice a year, for a week in the summer and during the Christmas holidays.

Despite their prosperity, Alfred and Mildred Phillips had decided long ago they preferred a small but well-appointed house for themselves and their son. So they settled on a log cabin, built sturdily, with a wooden shingle roof. Inside were a parlor, kitchen, dining room, two bedrooms and a small office used by both of the Phillips to conduct business, coordinate their good works, and for the occasional crochet project that Mildred relaxed with. The office also served as a guest room when extra relatives came to visit.

The rooms were filled with expensive furniture and accessories, including antiques from Europe and some art work the couple had purchased on a trip to England and France.

Peshtigo

But their oasis in the forest was now threatened by the occasional fires and smoke that affected the entire region. The normally-upbeat couple was now concerned about the future of their property. A trip to Chicago, planned for early October to visit relatives, was canceled as the situation deteriorated and Alfred determined he could not leave his place while the fire danger persisted.

"There will always be time to visit Chicago," he told his wife. "The city will be there forever and your relatives should be there for several years to come. We can go when the rains return and it's safe to leave our land."

*   *   *

Henry Bateman labored tirelessly and endlessly in Lower Sugar Bush. He had to because there were eight mouths to feed in the Bateman family. Henry was a Wisconsin dairy farmer with twenty Holsteins to feed and milk every single day of the year.

The Batemans owned fifty acres of land, nearly all of it grazing land for the cows. There was a large barn with a side-room used to store milk until it was taken to market in Green Bay, where it was pasteurized or processed into butter and cheese. Henry also had two outbuildings holding equipment, wagons, and stalls for the horses which pulled the wagons.

The Bateman home was several hundred feet from the barn. When Henry first built the house, it was modest in size. But as his family mushroomed, so did the house, one addition after another.

Henry Bateman was thirty-six years old, yet he looked fifteen years older. He operated his dairy farm almost singlehandedly, employing just two farm workers who lived in Lower Sugar Bush. Henry had always known it was a demanding business, milking twice a day, moving the animals into and out of the barn, rounding them up in the pastures, preserving their health and safety, feeding them promptly, storing milk, and getting it sent to market. For the head of the Bateman household there were no days off, no slack periods, and no vacations. Even Sunday was not a day of rest, merely a day of less work. The Sunday service and the Sunday dinner provided the respite from the back-breaking, muscle-tensing work.

Henry had run his farm for years on his own. It was only after he had the business operating efficiently that he began to seek human companionship. He met a young, attractive, and articulate woman at his church. For months he courted Elizabeth Green, finally marrying her in 1859 in the same church where they first met.

Elizabeth understood that a life with Henry Bateman meant isolation from the town she had lived in with her family and it meant never-ending work as wife, companion, and co-worker on the farm. Such a life signaled almost certain deprivation. She also knew that life with Henry would include a large family because he had told her as much during their courtship. So, much of her time was spent carrying, and caring for, children, as well as milking and feeding cows but she came to love the life as much as she loved her humble husband.

The eldest of the offspring, Joshua Bateman, was ten and assisted his father as much as he could. He helped feed the cows each morning before rushing off to school and he helped feed them again just before the family's dinner. Daughter Louise was a year younger and aided her mother in the multitude of household chores. Henry Junior, who was called Hank, was seven and sister Maria was six. The babies in the family were three-year-old Walter and his younger-by-a-year brother Raymond.

Henry Bateman was pleased with his brood and happy to have achieved one of his life goals: a big family. And he felt confident the future of his farm was secure. As the boys grew, they could take on added responsibilities and, Henry hoped, at least one of them would carry on the work of the dairy when Henry retired.

But there was little time to contemplate the future because Henry Bateman's immediate concern was the safety of his family, his livestock, and his livelihood–all of which were threatened by the encroaching fires that smoldered off in the woods. Henry had heard from neighbors that several acres of forest were being consumed by flames farther west. Four days ago he decided to determine for himself the seriousness of the danger. He had taken his horses and a wagon west of the Sugar Bush settlement on a Sabbath Day after church services. But this was no typical Sunday drive. For several hours he scanned the distant horizon. When he returned home late that afternoon, he offered a grim assessment to his wife as they sat at the kitchen table, sipping strong black coffee.

"I saw perhaps a dozen separate fires out there. The cool autumn air was being cooked by fire. The sky was filled with a dense, suffocating smoke, blocking my vision for miles. The sun was shining through the smoke with a red angry glare. I am certain conditions are much more dangerous than a week ago."

When he finished his report, his wife sat speechless, motionless. Tears welled up in her eyes. After several minutes of silence, Elizabeth Bateman took a long drink of still-steaming coffee.

"Good God!" she exclaimed. "We're doomed."

Chapter 4

October 6, 1871.

He had concluded his morning prayers in the chapel of his small house in the center of Peshtigo. Now, over a lunch of cheese, an apple, and coffee, Father Peter Pernin wrote in his diary about the swiftly deteriorating conditions he had witnessed the previous day in the woods outside of town.

"The forests were tinder, ready, even anxious for the destructive force of fire," he wrote. "All God's creation seems so dry and miserable, it almost cries out for death. God protect us and save us, as we remain in your loving care. But give us the courage to persevere in the face of adversity. Amen."

The Roman Catholic priest's rectory adjoined the still-uncompleted Church at the corner of Oconto and Ellis Avenues. Workers had completed the steepled bell-tower and the inside of the main sanctuary was ready for plastering. Ceiling beams were in place and Father Pernin hoped and prayed the roof would be constructed before winter. The congregation gathered in the roofless Church each Sunday for Mass. No one was worried that the service would be disrupted by rain. Father Pernin had earlier considered that a blessing but now the drought conditions seemed something of a cruel curse. The fire, smoke, and smoldering embers from the woodlands posed more serious dangers to the congregants than rain, even a soaking shower.

Father Pernin served two parishes. In Marinette, less than ten miles northeast of Peshtigo, he had a church and residence, supported by a strong and stable community twice as large as the Peshtigo parish. A third building was under construction, which was slated to become a parish school. But as Peshtigo's population grew, the priest realized he had to build an edifice for his parishioners there. That task was nearly accomplished.

In recent weeks the Sunday mass had been packed. The priest saw his flock swell as drought conditions worsened. The number of distant fires increased and the choking smoke thickened. The public's recent attitude was a marked change from a month earlier. Father Pernin had used his Sunday sermon as a type of bully pulpit.

"God forgive us," he bellowed, his oratory bouncing off the church walls, "the saloons are open, the men are inside drinking and shouting, even as our town is threatened by smoke and flames. The smoke-filtered rays of the sun have cast a sickly yellow light across Peshtigo."

But the ignorance, or nonchalance, of the townspeople slowly gave way to tensions and outright fear. Father Pernin could detect it in the faces of his communicants, not only at Sunday Mass but also outside the church. He prayed each day for deliverance from the fires for himself and his flock. Still, he reconciled himself to the possibility that a major blaze could destroy not just his church and presbytery but much of his community as well, along with many of its people. His optimistic nature reminded him the church was just two blocks from the Peshtigo River, which would choke off any fires that approached from the north or east and spare his house of worship. His pessimistic side felt certain fires would blow into town from the prevailing westerly winds and destroy his property.

Because he was a practical man, Peter Pernin decided he must secretly prepare for the worst. Several days earlier, he had gone to a place between the church and the rectory. He dug a hole three feet deep and two across. The priest then inserted a metal box in the cavity. He covered the box lightly with sand and Wisconsin soil and then placed a few large stones over the loosely-packed mixture. Father Pernin's mission was clear: he needed to protect his most valuable possessions in case of uncontrolled fire. He had taken his gold chalice, used to hold the wine which he consecrated into the blood of Jesus Christ at the mass, the silver cross that stood upon the altar, and the relic of a saint kept in the altar and placed them inside the container. By preparing this sepulcher ahead of time, he hoped to salvage the significant artifacts of his Church ministry, even if the building were destroyed. One other precious item, the tabernacle which held consecrated hosts, would be left inside the church. Should fire approach, Father Pernin vowed to retrieve it and carry it to safety.

Peter Pernin was a native of France. He was born Pierre Pernin. His father repaired shoes and made new ones from a small shop in a small village. His mother took in washing and supervised her six children. The Pernins were deeply religious so when their second son said he wanted to become a priest, the family felt it had been blessed.

After years of prayer, study, and training, Peter was ordained a priest. He served a few years in his native land, then decided to emigrate to the United States. His first assignment was the rural recesses of Northern Wisconsin, in Marinette on the Menominee River, and later in Peshtigo. Moving to Marinette presented a test of faith for the young priest but Father Pernin rose to the challenge. Despite the isolation and occasional loneliness of his backwoods posting, he had made great strides in developing his two congregations, building churches and a school, and in getting to know, as well as serving, his parishioners.

But now his faith was being tested as clouds of smoke drifted across Peshtigo and word spread of forest fires coming closer to the community. With each new week, it became more difficult to encourage his flock that the town and its people would be saved from the ravages of a major fire.

Upon completing his diary entry, Father Pernin turned his attention to his Sunday sermon. He prayed for inspiration, knowing that crowds of the faithful would fill his church pews, seeking solace and comfort. He prayed he would be able to motivate and guide them, as their worries rose.

*   *   *

Maybell Kittner had no time for fear. She had become accustomed to the fetid odor of the fires and smoke. She was matriarch of a large extended family. Maybell Kittner was responsible for her own three children, her widowed mother Mary, her younger sister Nan, and Nan's three children - all of whom lived under one roof in her home on the western edge of Peshtigo.

Like her mother, Maybell was a widow. Her husband Clyde had been a strong and strong-willed lumberman who spent winter after winter felling trees in the forests of Northern Wisconsin and Northwestern Michigan. He had risen from being a saw-man to field boss and was in charge of an entire camp of shanty boys. This assignment required that he remain in the backwoods with his men during the week but he returned to his home and family every weekend. His camp was about thirty miles outside of town. On many Friday nights he traveled with one or more of his workers, as they made tracks to Peshtigo for a weekend of drinking and debauchery in the bars and brothels. And on several Sundays, he returned to the woods with some of his men after their debilitating but presumably satisfying two days in town. When harvest season ended each spring, Clyde Kittner moved into his home full-time and worked in The Peshtigo Company woodenware plant.

His underlings in the logging camp called Clyde indestructible but one day he was destroyed, deep in the woods he loved so dearly and which provided him and his family a comfortable living.

He had been supervising a crew of shanty boys cutting pines not far from Upper Sugar Bush, in thick forest between the Peshtigo and Menominee Rivers. A two-man crew had completed sawing a monstrous tree and it began to topple. Unexpectedly, a gust of wind blew in at the very moment the tree began to tip toward earth, taking the tree away from its intended trajectory. Before he could fully comprehend what was happening, let alone outrun the mammoth pine, it crashed down on him, knocking him to the ground, and crushing him instantly.

It took more than a day for the lumber company to respond to the scene of the tragedy, confirm Clyde Kittner's death, then notify Maybell of the tragedy. Overcome by grief Maybell took comfort in knowing that her husband had loved his work and would rather have died in the forest than anyplace else. And although the routine they had come to know offered a certain comfort to Maybell, Clyde's death unsettled her greatly. Even as she was nursing a morbid sense of loss, her children seemed far more resilient. Because they had seen their father only on weekends during the wood-cutting season, Maybell concluded the youngsters were conditioned to his long absences and to accept his final absence. Eventually, over time and over many tears, Maybell herself came to realize that she must accept her fate and move her life forward.

She adopted a new attitude, becoming tougher since she knew she could no longer count on her husband to handle the hardy chores or do the heavy lifting. She accepted that Clyde would not be there to help in raising the children, that he would not be available for home repairs. Maybell Kittner knew it was now up to her to protect herself and her children, Asa, Richard, and Clair. Just a few weeks before her husband's fatal accident, Maybell invited her mother to stay in the family's cramped cottage. Maybell needed some adult companionship and some occasional comforting, the kind only a mother can supply when a husband is absent. Mary Bartholomew proved to be the perfect guest. She provided her daughter with emotional sustenance and physical assistance with household responsibilities, from making meals, to mending clothes, to minding children.

About a month after Clyde's funeral, which was paid for by his employer, officials from the company paid a visit to Maybell Kittner one evening after supper. They informed her of an insurance policy they had issued Clyde when he first began work for the Peshtigo Company. Given the hazardous nature of lumbering, the firm covered all workers in the event of injury or death. The two company executives handed Maybell a check and extended their gratitude once more for the good work Clyde Kittner had performed for the company.

When the visitors departed, Maybell gazed in utter shock at the enormous amount of money she had just inherited. She decided then she would put the money to the most appropriate need she could imagine. She soon contacted builders about enlarging her small house. That would give her family ample room and would provide a special area for her mother, who could move in permanently. Maybell also invited her younger sister to join the family and made sure her expansion plans included enough bedrooms for the newcomers.

Like Maybell, Nan was a single mother. Unlike her sister, she was not a widow. Her husband, apparently despondent about his life and lack of prospects, left the family home one morning for work, never to return. Neither Nan nor her three children ever saw him again. Nan soldiered on bravely in the one-room house outside Oconto. She worked as a house cleaner for two wealthy Oconto families, the income barely covering the costs of housing, food, clothing, and other necessities. So when Maybell asked her sister to move into the enlarged Peshtigo house, Nan thanked her sister for her kindness and thanked God for her new good fortune.

Maybell Kittner's mother and sister eventually sold their respective properties and gave Maybell part of the proceeds toward the upkeep of the new home for the three adults and six children now living there.

The women had enough money to provide a comfortable living for the group. No one had to work outside the home. At the end of the day, when the children were tucked into their beds, the three adults would sit together, in the parlor during the cold months or on the front porch when the weather was warm. Over coffee, they would discuss their individual setbacks but glorify the good things that had come to them lately. They were together, their health was good, they were comfortable, and they were safe. Together, they agreed, they could face any adversity. In their numbers there was strength. Strength to overcome the drought and accompanying fears of fire. They knew God would protect them.

* * *

John Cox removed his apron, near the large sink at the rear of George Robinson's butcher shop in the center of Peshtigo. He had just closed the shop and was preparing to wash up after a day of dicing beef into steaks and ground meat, slicing pork into chops and roasts, and cutting up whole chickens. As he lathered his hands and wrists to remove the grease, blood, and fragments, John Cox exhaled a sigh of satisfaction. He had done a respectable day's work serving the needs of his customers; he looked forward to having the next two days off work.

It was Mr. Robinson's week to open the shop on Saturday, so John would get Friday and Saturday off for rest and relaxation, although he reminded himself neither would be truly possible as long as this fire threat continued to envelope the community.

John was twenty-four years of age, single, and dedicated to his work, or at least to the idea that this work would lead to a brighter future. He saved a large portion of his weekly earnings, which he put away with two goals clearly in focus. He would use his savings to buy or build a house, allowing him to leave the furnished efficiency unit in a local rooming house near the Peshtigo River that he now called home. The remainder of the money would provide the necessary capital to start his own business. John Cox wanted to sell men's and women's clothing.

He had moved to Peshtigo a few years earlier from Racine, in Southern Wisconsin. He'd grown up there but decided it was time to move on, away from his family. Given the booming business in the north, he made his way to Green Bay but continued to Peshtigo after hearing about the prosperity related to the lumber industry. As he got his bearings in the community, he watched the shanty boys at work and at play. John determined that was not for him. He knew he preferred to work at a business in the town so he could get to know it and its people better. He also wanted to learn the fundamentals of operating and owning a business. John found an opening at Robinson's butcher shop, after a half-dozen other shopkeepers turned him down for various reasons.

John Cox was grateful for the opportunity and, as time passed, the relationship between the journeyman butcher and his employer blossomed. George had become a mentor and father-figure to the young man far from home, with few friends. In turn, John returned the loyalty by working tirelessly for the business. He earned a respectable wage and also got to take home free meat and poultry for preparation in his tiny kitchen. John could tell his family and friends back home in Racine that he was enjoying his new life and was prospering as Peshtigo continued to grow and prosper.

When he didn't work in the shop, John Cox enjoyed spending time with his only two friends who, like him, were unmarried. As he dried his hands, John thought about tonight's planned gathering of the threesome at a local tavern for dinner and a few beers.

His other enjoyment was practicing the bow and arrow. Practice had made perfect because John was an excellent shot and a keen hunter. He seldom missed an opportunity to spend at least an hour on his day off sending arrows screaming into a target on the side of a tree at the edge of town.

And John Cox was developing a new passion, albeit slowly. He had started to search for eligible young women. The time had come, he decided, to start courting.

Peshtigo

As he locked the front door of the butcher shop for the night and headed to his apartment, John walked past an attractive young woman with enticing red hair. He did not know Kate Guillfoyle, who had just completed her own day's work in the office of the Peshtigo Company's cranberry operation. The young beauty was looking forward to a quiet night at home, first with a bowl of soup, then curled up with the new book she was reading. Kate was twenty-two and lived alone. She had moved north from Milwaukee just a few months earlier to escape what she considered the overcrowded and overly-sinful big city. Kate was religious, attending Sunday mass each week at Father Pernin's soon-to-be-completed Catholic church. She also helped with church chores and often brought the priest some prepared meals for his dinner.

After passing John Cox, Kate coughed a bit, then sneezed. Smoke had apparently lodged in her throat and nose.

John Cox turned immediately. "God bless you, ma'am."

"Why, thank you," was Kate's initial reply. "This relentless smoke is taking its toll, at least on my nose."

"Yes ma'am," responded John. "I hope conditions improve, for the sake of your nose."

As he smiled, she laughed.

"Well, good night," she said.

"Good night to you."

Each of them turned and resumed their initial course.

*   *   *

Elias Dix was walking home from his work at the Peshtigo Company's woodenware plant. The haze which had precipitated Kate Guillfoyle's sneeze also embedded itself deep in Dix's throat. He cleared it continually, much to his own annoyance, as he trudged home. Elias had lived in Northern Wisconsin all his life. His parents resided outside Peshtigo and were grain farmers. But Elias realized early on he wanted nothing to do with agriculture. He sought a job that had a defined start-time and end-time for each day's labor. Farmers often worked several hours per day, or several days straight during certain times of the year. And Elias wanted work that provided secure and steady income. Farming had its boom years and bust years. In fact, the current dry spell was proving to be troublesome for farmers like his father.

Elias Dix began working at the Peshtigo Company after finishing his studies at the local school. He remained at home while he saved money for his own property. At the same time, he had been courting a young woman who also worked for the company and lived at home with her family as well.

Her name was Rachel Cartwright, an only child. When the time came for Elias and Rachel to announce their engagement, it became clear that her mother did not agree to any plan which would take her daughter away from her. But the couple was patient and persistent. In time, Rachel's mother became not only fond of the young Mister Dix but also quite happy with the prospect of a wedding. A few months later, and with the blessing of all the parents, Rachel Cartwright became Rachel Dix in the Peshtigo Congregational Church.

In the interim, Elias had built a home in the town, not far from the couple's joint workplace. The two walked to work together each morning but returned home at different times. She left earlier and had time to prepare dinner before Elias got there.

Rachel continued working until she became pregnant. The birth of the first Dix baby led to a rapid succession of other births. There were two boys, followed by three girls.

Now, as Elias headed home on this smoky Friday evening, he thought about his youngsters and wondered whether the deplorable conditions were jeopardizing their health. Abram Dix was nine, his brother Martin a year younger. The eldest girl, Catherine, was six, followed by four-year old Iris, and finally the baby of the family, two-year-old Catelin.

Elias Dix was still about four blocks from home when he became aware of a great noise building steadily behind him. As he turned to identify the cause of the commotion, a horse-drawn fire pumper came careening by. Several men carrying buckets or blankets followed the wagon, running as fast as they could, but slowing, because of the distance they had traveled already. Elias noticed the frantic look on many of their faces.

A minute later, a second wagon raced by. The driver was lashing the two horses and screaming at them above the din, exhorting the beasts to rush faster, pull harder. Some of the firemen-on-foot were shouting, urging each other to continue running until they reached their destination.

Elias Dix stood motionless during this high-decibel display. Then he was jolted into the realization that the firefighters were racing in the very direction of his home. Standing still gave way to high-speed sprinting. It took just a few minutes to arrive at his home and when he did so, he was relieved. Neither his house nor property was affected by the fire. Still, he could see the smoke and flames from blazes that appeared not too far distant. Hugh yellow-orange flames shot high into the air, licking at trees. A gust of wind blew up, and Elias became cognizant of another painful truth. The wind was blowing from the West, pushing the flames in the direction of his property.

Another wagon clattered past his house.

"Good God!" Elias exclaimed. His fear rose that this fire, or series of fires, could reach his house and destroy it. He ran inside, collected his wife and children, and had them assemble on the front porch. As each family member emerged, he or she brought out wooden pails, products of the Peshtigo Company woodenware warehouse.

The family had done practice drills before, what to do if fire should threaten their house and yard. Elias must decide when to wet the house, making it more difficult for the fire to consume the all-wood structure. With water in short supply, he did not want to act hastily, waste water, and then watch the blaze change direction, moving away from the neighborhood.

"We shall save the water for now," he announced to his family, "until the fire threatens the house which, praise the Lord, it will not do."

Neighbors were engaged in the same pursuits. Families had left their dwellings and stood clear, in case flames should reach their homes and create great walls of fire. Men gathered in groups, assessing the situation and the weather. They made educated guesses on the fire's progress. No one thought it necessary to water down his house, at least not yet.

Rachel Dix walked closer to her youngest children. Catelin and Iris were crying. All the family members had trouble breathing normally but the smoke and haze were especially frightening to the little ones. Elias approached Rachel, suggesting she might take the children back to the house. He promised he would remain on constant vigil outside. He told his wife to close all the windows on the west-facing side of the house, while opening windows on the other side slightly to allow some ventilation. He also advised them to lie on the floor, where they would be less likely to inhale the heavy smoke. As he said that, he began to cough, having taken in extra smoke while giving his instructions. The rest of the family moved slowly back inside the wooden frame house.

Elias moved the buckets closer to the large barrels which normally caught rain water but lately had to be filled with water from the almost-dry creek nearby. There were two receptacles at the front of the Dix house, each about three-quarters full. Elias knew that if a huge fire blew toward his house, the water in those barrels would be insufficient to save the structure but a small, stray fire might be snuffed out with the water available. He peered through the smoke to check the status of the blaze.

Firemen fanned out to attack the flames. The biggest fire wagon positioned itself between one blaze and the town center. Several men circled the wagon, some attaching a fire hose, others preparing to pump water from inside the wagon.

The second vehicle went to confront another blaze, just as the third wagon arrived. It had the smallest tank, thus the fewest gallons of water to tamp down this blaze. The men on the ground barked orders among themselves, while stomping flames with their feet and smothering flames with their blankets and brooms.

Just as one fire was suppressed, another lick of flame flared elsewhere. The ground was so hot it generated new fires and the wind whipped the flames along the parched earth. To combat this, some men carried buckets of water from the pumper wagon and tried to dampen the hot spots and prevent further outbreaks.

At the first wagon, the pumping team was moving furiously and water was spraying from the main fire hose, held by four men, who directed the flow toward the moving flames. Initially, it appeared the fire was too intense, traveling too quickly, to be tamed by their timid jet of water. As some pumped and others pointed the nozzle, the men shouted encouragement to one another, entreating the pumpers not to give up until they could get the flames in check. The water eventually did its job and the firefighters were able to put out the flames. Left behind were thick, billowy clouds of dense smoke. At a signal from one hose-holder, the men astride the wagon ceased pumping. Exhausted, many dropped to the ashen ground to rest.

The second team was facing a more serious blaze. The men had to pump longer and harder. One factor was the fire's location, near a stand of pine trees. The wind blew flames quickly along the dry ground, and when the fire encountered a dry tree stump, it seemed to attack. The flames appeared to rush up the sides of a few trees as the desiccated wood seemed to drink in the fire, conducting them up the shaft to the dry, dead leaves or pine needles. This new fuel energized the fire. Three trees became engulfed in flame in a matter of seconds. The heat became so intense, one of them exploded before the firemen's eyes. The men jumped back in horror. Sparks were hurled to the ground, setting new tiny blazes. The men ran to the new outbreaks and tried to stifle them before they could do any damage.

The wagon driver, sensing the danger, moved in closer to bring water to the growing inferno. Once the wagon was in its new position, several men returned to their pumping bars. They resumed pumping with almost superhuman vigor. The men holding the hose sprayed the trees in an effort to control the spread of the fire. After what seemed like an eternity, the flames surrounding one tree went out. The other tree was more fully involved and it took several more minutes to extinguish that blaze. Just as the fire was snuffed out, the firemen realized they had drained the wagon of its precious cargo. But at least the flames were finished, the fires were out.

The last group was still involved, unable to quell what looked like the smallest and most benign of the blazes. The first wagon, which still contained water, joined the fray. Once it stopped, the men reversed roles. Those who had been on the hose line went to pump, while the pumpers took their places directing the water flow.

The last fire was spreading rapidly, extending beyond the reach of the pumper's hose. Men and a few women tied handkerchiefs around their faces to minimize smoke damage to noses and lungs. It did little to prevent the smoke from affecting their eyes, which were red and watery. The women and men ran through the flaming field, beating down new flames as they burst out of the tinder dry grass. They employed blankets, brooms, boots, and water buckets. And eventually they succeeded. They had managed to rob the flames of their sustenance. The fires were out.

In the smokey haze, there was now an eerie silence. Spread out before the tired firefighters were charred trees, blackened grass, and white-hot ash. A thick pallid smoke lay just above their heads. Those who had gathered to fight the flames could finally relax. They were too tired to cheer their victory, or even to savor it fully. They merely stood or sat, catching their collective breath, thanking their God and their friends for once again forestalling a tragedy.

When there was general agreement that the danger had passed, they began dispersing. The wagons were returned to the fire station near the town center. Other people came forward to clean the vehicles and begin the arduous task of refilling the pumper tanks. Another group washed, dried, fed and calmed the horses who had carried the wagons to the fire scene so swiftly, then endured hours of heat, flames, smoke, and trauma.

At his own house, Elias Dix uttered his own prayer of thanksgiving and sighed in utter relief. He could no longer see the brightness in the sky, so he knew the fire had been put out. He also noted that the smoke was rising, a sure sign to him there were no more flames. He rose to his feet, having no idea how long he'd been sitting on his front porch, ready to defend his life, his family, and his home had the fire approached.

Then he heard the fire wagons pass through the area and he knew the danger must be over. He went to the corners of the house, retrieved the wooden buckets, and carried them into the house. It was dark and quiet inside.

"Rachel," he whispered.

"Here, dear," she replied. She fumbled a bit in the dark, then struck a wooden match and lit a candle. In the dim light, Elias Dix could distinguish his five children, lying close together, fast asleep on the parlor floor.

"I think the fires are out," he told Rachel.

"God be praised," she said.

"We have been fortunate tonight," Elias added. "But without rain, our trees and grasses, even this wooden home, will become an inferno. And perhaps the next time, the men will not be able to put it out."

"Have faith, Elias, we managed to survive this assault. With strength and courage, we will survive the next one," she told her husband.

"It was good you closed the windows," he said. "It is less smoky in here than outside."

"Still, the stress has affected all the children," she told him. "They cried themselves to sleep and I feel quite tired myself."

"Yes and I am weary too. We need to sleep and hope for a better day tomorrow."

Rachel Dix, candle in hand, led the way to their bedroom. They decided to leave the children as they were, rather than disturb or unnerve them.

They had survived another day of drought and fire. Neither would admit it but they wondered how long their good fortune would last.

Chapter 5

October 7, 1871.

Hellfire and brimstone.

In the town of Marinette, another revival meeting was planned. For the past three weeks, a local group had been conducting the sessions and attendance had been growing steadily. The first revival meeting was organized after fires broke out near the town. Those responsible for these religious gatherings had opted for the hellfire theme, deeming them appropriate in light of the current conditions in Northern Wisconsin.

This port community on the Wisconsin bank of the Menominee River was the first parish community of Father Peter Pernin. The priest had managed to build a church, a presbytery, and a school for his flock which came from Marinette and from its sister-town Menominee, across the river in Michigan.

The area had developed rapidly as the timber industry grew in size and scope. Wood was brought to the waterfronts of each town, where it was loaded onto ships which took it either to the city of Green Bay or down Lake Michigan to Milwaukee and Chicago. Marinette was larger than Peshtigo at one time and had a more lively collection of shops, bars, and restaurants. But as Peshtigo prospered, many Marinette merchants opened second stores along the Peshtigo River.

Marinette also had its own newspaper, the *Eagle*, which served the region. It reported community news along with bits of gossip, including a story in the September 5th edition about a local woman who had given birth to another baby, her twenty-third child.

The *Eagle* had a major story to cover in the dog days of 1871. The paper reported extensively on the drought that plagued all of Northern Wisconsin and Northwest Michigan and its impact on the various communities. On September 30th, the *Eagle* told readers "the fires have nearly died out now in this vicinity."

Many residents of Marinette, Peshtigo, and other towns breathed a sigh of relief. While there were no signs of rain, at least the local journal was telling them there were no forest fires to fear in the vast wilderness that surrounded them. Such news accounts led many to believe the worst was over, that life was returning to normal, that they needn't worry about fire danger. But there were countless others in the region who refused to believe the news story. And there was evidence that blazes were continuing to break out. That's why so many people gathered for the prayer meetings, putting their faith in God Almighty and not the Marinette *Eagle*.

But the paper's earlier assessment of the fire situation turned out to be flawed. And in the October 7th edition, the news took an entirely different tack.

"Fires are still raging all over the county. The raw air of autumn is being well cooked by fire. The thick smoke has been tough on mosquitos. We in Marinette now breathe a little easier. However, Peshtigo is yet very far from being out of danger. Unless we have rain soon, God knows how soon a conflagration may sweep the town," the *Eagle* wrote.

When Peshtigo readers got the news, they became even more unsettled. But even in Marinette, there was unease. In truth, blazes continued burning in the vast forests south and west of Peshtigo and Oconto. Other fires smoldered west of Menominee and Marinette. And even though all four of these communities were located on rivers, residents knew they were not immune to fire damage. There was a report from just three days earlier that boat captains on the Green Bay reported the smoke was so thick over the water, they had difficulty navigating their ships. One skipper decided to drop anchor in the middle of the Bay, feeling it safer to be far from shore than crashing into other ships, docks, or coastlines. Other craft remained at anchor in Green Bay and Marinette rather than risk an accident.

The fires, smoke, and haze were not confined to the western side of the Green Bay. On the eastern peninsula, residents endured the same hardships and harbored the same fears about the weather and the prospects for something worse. The townsfolk of Sturgeon Bay and Williamsonville watched smoke come from both directions, from fires off to the west which blew a haze across the Bay and obscured the towns. But other blazes on the eastern peninsula created their own smoke, which was blown from Lake Michigan in the east, back across the towns. The danger extended south to the town of New Franken, not far from the city of Green Bay.

Williamsonville, in Door County, was another company town of the timber industry. It had been settled by the Williams brothers, who developed and built a lumber mill, hired workers to fell trees and mill the logs brought to town. It was located at the mouth of an inlet so the wood could easily be loaded onto ships and carried away to markets farther south.

Compared to Peshtigo and Marinette, Williamsonville was still small but it was on the move. The town had its own general store and post office, operated by the mill company. It had a church, a carpentry/blacksmith operation, a large rooming house, and a bar-restaurant combination. All were located near the town's most important assets, the mill and the dock.

Like its neighbors, Williamsonville was covered in wood and its detritus. Every building in the village was built from wood, from floor to roof. The main street was dirt, which had become dust as the dry spell deepened but along each side of the thoroughfare were wooden walkways. And all around the Williams brothers' mill were mountains of wood tailings, piled as high as buildings. Recent winds had scattered the wood chips, blowing them in mini-piles nears homes and businesses. As the fire danger mushroomed, homeowners and shopkeepers alike took pains to sweep away the dry wooden bits to reduce the risk of damage or destruction in case of fire.

There were seventy-six souls living in the town in the autumn of 1871: Forty-five men, fifteen women, and some sixteen children. The males were, for the most part, shanty-boys, who spent their days denuding forests and their nights and weekends drinking and dining at the bar or the hotel. Some of the lumbermen had families to support, so their off-hours were spent at home with wives and children.

Williamsonville was so isolated that virtually everyone in the town knew everyone else. The loftiest lumber barons mingled with the lowliest shanty-boys and the families. The women were perhaps the closest, forming small clubs and cliques, but gathering en masse for social occasions. The women helped each other with chores, large and small, as well as the birthing of babies and the laying out of the dead. Two of Williamsonville's women acted as school teachers, instructing the children, who were old enough, in their reading and writing. Classes were held in the women's homes. Others took responsibility for organizing community social events and worked closely with the minister on religious events, and cleaned the church on a regular basis.

The townspeople laughed together during the good times and wept together in times of tragedy. They clung together now, as fears rose about the risk of devastating wildfires. As a community, they had endured the months of drought and its impact on their lives. Together they suffered the more recent misery of acrid, choking smoke which had been draped over their village. While they knew of no major fires near them, they heard stories of the rash of blazes on both sides of the Green Bay. Mariners who docked at the inlet or travelers who arrived on horseback, wagon, or even on foot via the single rutted road from New Franken, told them of forest fires and resulting fears. As a group, the people of Williamsonville were frightened. The mill owners, businessmen, and residents took precautions. They placed water barrels at various intervals on the streets and near the wooden structures. Residents loosened the earth or dug ditches around their homes. The exposed dirt, they hoped, would act as a fire retardant. Brooms and blankets and buckets were positioned on porches, to beat and smother fires that might break out.

Each Sunday, after church, townspeople gathered to exchange information on weather and ground conditions. They plotted strategy in the event fires should develop. They would have to fight the flames themselves because Williamsonville had no fire equipment. The residents were the firefighters. Just two years ago, all the residents had not only banded together to quell a fire at a neighbor's home but they had later regrouped to help rebuild the damaged structure.

But this was different. They knew that if things continued to worsen, all of their homes and stores could be damaged or destroyed. They had to be ready.

* * *

"It is so dry down New Franken way," said Silas Masterson to some of the other men in a small circle, "folks there say fires could break out at any time. All it will take is a big spark and a gust of wind and then we will have a fire on our hands."

Peter Magdeburg shook his head.

"If a fire like that should develop, there is little or nothing we could do to stop it from rolling right through this little town and burning everything in its path."

"In that case, what each family must do is make a break for the Bay and get into the water," suggested Oral Mingus.

Daniel Haney listened to his neighbors before speaking.

"We have survived this dry nightmare for so long. And I have prayed every day that God protect us, bring us rain, spare us a major catastrophe. That is still my prayer but the news we get from the south and the west alarms me. I fear our fortunes may change, for the worse. I hope I am wrong and God will deliver us from danger. And I pray He will bring us rain."

Chapter 6

J.F. Kelsey had been a busy man of late. Peshtigo's only physician and the co-owner of the town apothecary was seeing a larger-than-normal number of patients in his office and his pharmacy. He was also making many more house calls than normal, including the one to Priscilla Maxon just a few days earlier.

Each night, when there was no more call for his services, Doctor Kelsey would sit at his office desk, a wing of his Peshtigo home, and make entries in his log book. He listed the people he had seen that day, their ailments, the drugs he may have prescribed, and the amount his clients had paid him. Most could afford his professional advice and the medications he ordered for them. These customers paid in cash. Others paid in kind, with firewood, vegetables, a plucked chicken, a pair of woolen mittens. And a few patients could not pay at all. J.F. Kelsey always said the same thing to them.

"Pay me when you can, I know you will not forget."

The physician had noticed that over the past several weeks, not only had his patient-load increased but he was seeing a disturbing trend in maladies. Patients had come down with more coughs and colds than was common for October. For others it was worse, as they displayed signs of wheezing, bronchitis, and pneumonitis, their lungs burning. Children complained of sore and watery eyes, their noses seemed to run constantly. The elderly seemed more incapacitated, afraid to leave their homes. People ran more frequent fevers. They were listless.

Doctor Kelsey noted that with the rise in physical problems, there was a concomitant increase in mental problems. More and more people were depressed. He knew it was the weather. The long drought, the smoke and haze, and the few close-call fires were making people ill. And the constant worries about more smoke and haze and fires were making them emotional wrecks.

These were difficult days for a country doctor, far from the nearest hospital in Green Bay. On more than one occasion, J.F. Kelsey wondered about the increased ailments and his ability to treat his patients and to cope with their conditions. He often felt disconsolate himself, trying to maintain his own physiological and psychological health, while watching his neighbors getting sick in both body and spirit. And there was no one to whom he could confide about the increased illnesses. His professional oath forbade him from discussing his patients' conditions. And he could not bring himself to tell friends and associates that the current climatic conditions were beginning to worry him as much as others in Peshtigo.

This should have been the best of times for Doctor Kelsey. His increased patient traffic had increased his income. And the medicines he prescribed patients meant his apothecary was reaping financial rewards. So many drugs were being purchased that he had to send almost daily orders to his pharmaceutical supplier in Green Bay.

John Frederick Kelsey was not a religious man, at least he had not been until recently. But he found himself going to the Congregational Church over the past two Sundays. He was not even sure he knew how to pray. But he felt a certain comfort being with his friends and neighbors in the church, praying for deliverance and singing hymns he had learned as a boy. And he relished the greetings he received before and after the Sunday service from those he had helped, even those he had not.

"Good morning, Doctor Kelsey," they would say to him. "So nice to see you."

"Thank you, doctor, for what you have done for me."

"I feel much better now after those pills you prescribed."

"Doc, you are a miracle worker; now if you could just do something about the weather."

He had come to Peshtigo five years ago, by way of Green Bay and Boston. John Kelsey had grown up in Concord, Massachusetts, one of two sons from a wealthy and eccentric family. Thomas Kelsey was a silversmith in Concord and his thriving business had allowed him a full and comfortable life. The senior Kelsey was able to hire apprentices who did the work, allowing him leisure time to count the money and enjoy it. His wife Emily had borne him two sons. And they made an unusual decision in naming their progeny. The first boy was named after Thomas' father and Emily's father. He was christened Frederick John Kelsey. The second son was given the same two names, only in reverse order. He was John Frederick.

Peshtigo

The older boy grew up called Fred, the younger brother was known as Johnny. He was three years younger than his big brother.

Fred Kelsey was accepted at Harvard College in Cambridge and decided to study law. He excelled in his classes and graduated near the top of his class. He decided to move into Boston to practice law. He bought a charming townhouse on Chestnut Street in Beacon Hill, which also served as his office.

Given the elder brother's success at Harvard, John Frederick was admitted to the college when he applied. But J.F. chose a different career path. He wanted to become a doctor.

After completing his undergraduate studies at the main campus in Cambridge, Johnny moved on to the Medical School in Boston proper, where he withstood the arduous hours of study and the longer hours of hospital internship. When he finally received his certificate to practice, the new Doctor Kelsey began his career at the Massachusetts General Hospital in Boston, a prestigious institution in a city which had distinguished itself in the practice of the healing arts. It was a mixed blessing for the young physician. He was a member of a renowned medical team in a first-rate facility in one of America's medical capitals. Yet J.F. Kelsey realized that he might remain an indistinguishable member of that elite group for many years to come. To spread out, and to stand out, he would have to consider another venue.

While reading some medical journals, he came across employment notices that advised of opportunities for physicians in the northern Midwest. While Chicago and Milwaukee had attracted competent medical professionals, the notices said there was a need for doctors in the northern part of Wisconsin and it mentioned the city of Green Bay specifically. John Kelsey made inquiries and in a series of letters, he agreed to join a new hospital in Green Bay.

It took him a few weeks to make his way to the rugged northern woods of Wisconsin. But once he set down his roots, Doctor Kelsey knew he had made the right choice. He was one of just four physicians at the hospital. His patient-load mushroomed and his reputation spread. He found that people came from remote towns and villages when they were ill because they had heard about the excellent doctors at the fine hospital in Green Bay.

Among his patients was the wife of one of Peshtigo's lumber lords. She spoke so highly of Doctor J. F. Kelsey that her husband talked with other local business leaders. They agreed that Peshtigo was growing and it needed the services of a capable doctor. The business leaders contacted J.F. Kelsey and made him a generous offer. If he would practice in Peshtigo, they would set him up with a house, which included a well-stocked office. As the town continued to grow and thrive, they promised Doctor Kelsey they would be prepared to build a small hospital and recruit doctors and nurses to staff it.

Johnny Kelsey was elated with the offer and relocated quickly to Peshtigo. One of the first people he met in his new hometown was Hiram Vierke, a local businessman. The two agreed to become partners in Peshtigo's first pharmacy. Doctor Kelsey soon realized he was cornering the market. He was the town's only doctor, prescribing medicines that could be purchased in only one pharmacy, his. And he was doing it with the blessings of his corporate benefactors.

Doctor Kelsey's practice thrived almost from the day he put out his shingle. At first, the bulk of his clients came from the Peshtigo Company's employees and their families. The firm had advised workers of the physician's presence in town and noted that the company had brought him to Peshtigo from Green Bay. But after an article in the *Eagle* and a healthy word-of-mouth campaign, it often seemed as though everybody in the community came to the doctor when he or she was sick.

J.F. Kelsey gave some of his patients medicine right in his office. For others, he wrote prescriptions. Hiram would fill them at their drug store.

After just a few months in Peshtigo, the new doctor had found his niche. He was a big fish in a small pond, working hard to help the sick, but a man who was becoming quite wealthy in his own right. He allowed himself two vacations each year. He took two weeks each August to travel. His recent holidays had taken him to Canada, the East Coast, and even a voyage to England, which lasted longer than two weeks. He also took a fortnight off during Christmas-time when he generally returned to Massachusetts to visit his family.

Peshtigo

Now, distressed by the long, dry summer and autumn and worn down by the recent hefty increase in his patient-load, Johnny Kelsey secretly craved the thought of this year's December vacation. He wanted to get away from this tinder box and these people who were tainted by the drought and its impact, both physically and emotionally. In fact, he had even contemplated staying in Concord a bit longer than just two weeks if weather conditions did not improve. Perhaps he'd stay in New England for an entire month. He just knew he needed a change of scenery.

*   *   *

Ten miles or so away, Terrence Kelly was on edge. The weather made him anxious. In fact, it made him more than that. It made him crazy. The ever-present dry conditions, the oppressive heat, even in October, the occasional fires and continuous smoky air combined to irritate Terrence Kelly.

His attitude affected his work and his family. The two were intertwined because he owned a farm in Upper Sugar Bush, so he worked where he lived. For weeks, it seemed to his wife Penelope that Terrence had been uncomfortable and, in turn, unpleasant to her and their four children.

He was upset because the lack of rain had all-but-withered his potato crop. The dead grass in his fields provided no food for his half-dozen dairy cows. A failed crop meant a failed income and unfed cows meant no milk for his family or his regular dairy customers.

In his anger and frustration, Terrence often took it out on his wife and the children. Malachy was nine and helped his father whenever and however he could. The boy assisted in milking the cows, when they had milk to give. He often helped plow the fields in spring and harvesting those fields in autumn. Aubrey, two years younger than Malachy, also helped his father any way his young arms and legs could. There were also two daughters. Charlotte was five and baby Molly was one. The older girl pretended to help her mother, particularly in minding her baby sister when Penelope had to wash clothes or prepare supper.

Terrence Kelly knew he was fretting too much about current conditions and knew he was being unkind to his own kin. Each week when the family went to Sunday services, he asked the Good Lord to give him courage to cope, to accept his fate, to forgive him for treating his family poorly, to make him more civil to those he loved the most. But a day or two later, the enormity of his problems overwhelmed him once more and he went on the attack again. He chastised the children, shouting at them, and on a few occasions striking them for no good reason. He would lose his temper over small things, and belittle his wife over trivial matters. After dinner some evenings, he would go for a walk on his land and come home crying over his present misfortunes. On days when he felt so distraught, he refused to get out of bed for breakfast and stayed in the bedroom until late in the morning.

Penelope had suggested he talk to the minister, or maybe he should pay a visit to the doctor in Marinette or Peshtigo. But Terrence repudiated all her overtures. In a fit of fury, he berated her in front of the children for suggesting he had a problem that required intervention by a doctor or a minister.

Terrence Kelly's constant worries led to a strain between himself and his wife, as well as the four children.

On this early October day, the temperature was nearly 80 degrees, it had not rained in a month, the air was heavy with heat and haze, and Terrence Kelly was sinking slowly but surely into a depression that only a break in the weather might relieve.

"I am not sure how much more of these conditions I can tolerate," he told his wife after lunch.

"My dear, I understand your concerns but you must calm yourself," responded his long-suffering mate. "There is little you or I can do about the weather. We can pray again tomorrow for relief. And you must pray again for help from the Almighty to help you overcome your frustration and your anger."

"I know, my dear," said Terrence Kelly. "I know how difficult I can be, how I treat you and the children. I will pray again for forgiveness, forbearance, and fortitude to rise above my basest instincts."

"I forgive you, but you must be gentle with the children. They cannot understand your meanness when they know they have done nothing wrong. These are difficult days, the most difficult since you and I were married and began our family. But this is not the time to lose faith and lash out against those who love you."

Terrence Kelly rose from the kitchen table, kissed his wife on the cheek, and left their wooden cabin.

He walked out into his fields, seeking solace in solitude. Everything Penelope had said was correct. And she had been saying it for weeks now. Why did he persist in his unpleasant behavior, when both he and his wife knew he was wrong?

Perhaps he was sick. Perhaps he needed help. As he walked, Terrence considered his options. He could not affect the weather but perhaps he could impact his own mental and physical health. He decided that he would visit the doctor one day next week. Perhaps he could help Terrence get back on an even keel.

Chapter 7

October 8, 1871.

The day of the Great Fire dawned as so many previous days had done. It was dry, warm, and hazy. But on this Sunday morning it was also still and calm. As the residents of Northern Wisconsin and Northwestern Michigan awoke on the Sabbath, they prepared for what they thought would be just another day in an endless pattern of drought.

What the people did not know was that as this Sunday progressed, an abnormal weather pattern would make it unique in Peshtigo's history and that of the United States. What residents could not know was that a monstrous Low Pressure System enveloped much of the country. It began as a sliver down the West Coast, then bulging outward from the Southwestern United States, up through the entire Midwest, and into the East Coast from Florida north into Vermont and New Hampshire.

The weather pattern brought unusually high temperatures, which would send the mercury near 80-degrees Fahrenheit in Northern Wisconsin, with low barometric pressure, about 29.50 in the northern woods. And as the day dragged on, winds would increase, gusting to as high as 30 miles per hour in the Northland's forested regions. Meteorologists would later describe a Cyclonic Storm that developed at 5:35 p.m. Central Time and which would, among other things, ignite a devastating blaze in Chicago and the disastrous fires in Wisconsin and Michigan. Others would term it an "atmospheric stream", which began in the Caribbean Sea in late August and blew into the Midwest in October with incredible force. The plain folks of this region who survived the inferno would not recall the event as a Cyclonic Storm or a gigantic Low Pressure System. They would call it simply a nightmare.

Across Peshtigo, there was movement in many directions. Families large and small began stirring. There were Sunday preparations, washing and dressing for church, making the morning meal, getting a start on the Sunday afternoon dinner. Beyond the town limits, the country dwellers went through a similar routine but added in morning chores, animals to feed, cows to milk, eggs to collect.

For many, a new day was beginning. For others, the night was just ending. For fast-living men without families or scruples, a long night of drinking, gambling, and womanizing was concluding. They had dragged themselves to their boarding houses, hotels, homes, and barns to sleep off their lascivious activities. Heat and haze played no part in their psyches. Whiskey, whores, and winning at cards were at the center of their lives. For the next several hours, they would be oblivious to the world beyond their beds.

The upright and upstanding citizens of the community soon began turning out for Sunday services. After another week of unforgiving weather, the venues were more crowded than ever.

So many worshipers packed into the Congregational Church, the rector decided against giving a sermon. Instead he led the crowd in a prayer for rain and then asked them to sing "Shall We Gather at the River". There was such a crowd at the Good Templars Hall for services of the Evangelical Lutheran Church that about fifty had to be turned away. The minister opened the Hall's windows wider so those outside could hear the proceedings.

The larger crowds at the Protestant services included Catholics. Because the unfinished Catholic church was about to be plastered, the altar, ornaments, and all the church pews had been removed. Father Peter Pernin had told his flock there would be no Mass and that he would visit his parishioners in Cedar River on this particular Sunday. Several of Father Pernin's parishioners begged him to remain in Peshtigo. The parish priest had tried to calm his constituents, telling them their fears were groundless and that they should trust in the Lord. A few of the people were placated but others remained uncertain and wary.

The faithful fulfilled their religious obligations despite the adversities. As the services concluded, pastors exchanged pleasantries with their congregants, encouraging them and comforting them. Men and women who had not seen each other for the past week attempted congenial conversation, putting aside their inner worries about the future even as the dry spell persisted. The good people of Peshtigo wished their friends and neighbors good health and good cheer. It was all that they could humanly do. The rest, they knew in their hearts, was up to their God.

With church finished for another week, it was time for relaxation, family reunions, and the Sunday roast. But the rising temperature combined with the heat from cooking fires made many kitchens uncomfortable for the women and girls preparing Sunday's special meal. The men and boys who played horseshoes in their yards or just sat on their porches awaiting their dinner found the conditions almost unbearable for October. Cooler weather should have moved in weeks ago and rain should have cleansed the dusty gardens and paths.

For some, there was a sense of foreboding, even a vague fear that something terrible was about to happen. For others, it was just another day off. By midday the bars were open and the revelers were back in operation. The food was palatable, the drinks were plentiful, and the women were playful. All were oblivious to outside weather conditions. This was the last day of the weekend, the last chance to enjoy life for another five days. Their thoughts were the same. Let us eat, drink, and be merry, for tomorrow we may die.

At 3 p.m., the temperature was close to 80 degrees. Most Peshtigans did not have a thermometer but they knew when they were hot. And they knew they were uncomfortably hot, in fact dangerously hot. A few folks looked skyward. Through the haze there were no clouds in sight. There was no chance of rain. Just more of the same. Surely, they said, this will end soon. It must end soon.

When the beef, pork, and ham suppers were finished and the dishes were done, families normally rested. A big meal often led to small naps on sitting room couches and front porch swings. But the post-meal respites were made more difficult by the uncomfortable conditions. Some families tried talking, others read aloud, still others gathered to tell stories but all did so in a glaze of perspiration as the heat permeated their surroundings.

On what was normally the liveliest time of the day, a silence settled over Peshtigo, a lethargy brought on by heat and hopelessness.

As early evening approached and the phenomenon called the Cyclonic Storm began to rumble across America's plains, Peshtigo remained quiet. It was the calm before the firestorm.

Peshtigo

* * *

"It has been too hot today," said many in the river town as the daylight dwindled and night came on.

What residents did not know at the time was that the temperature in Northern Wisconsin was as warm as the readings in Texas and Florida.

Hot, dry winds whipped through the region. These gusts were blowing from southwest to northeast. They moved at fourteen, then eighteen, and nineteen miles per hour but they were gusting at twenty-six and as much as thirty miles per hour. They were not cooling breezes. It was as though an invisible fire was spreading past people's faces, hands, and hair. People felt uncomfortably hot, almost as if they had been burned, although they could see no scars from the windy assault.

As Jeremiah Raymond and his wife Matilda strolled toward their wooden bungalow during their post-supper walk, they watched the last vestiges of a spectacular sunset. The haze-filled sky acted as a cloud-like filter. As the declining sun approached the horizon, its rays penetrated the haze and sent shimmers of blazing color across the western and southwestern sky. In better times, the Raymonds might have commented on the beauty of the moment. But lately, the ominous conditions had produced too many sunsets that were more frightening than fantastic.

"If I did not know better," Jeremiah said to his wife, "I would guess some forest fire is burning and heading this way."

* * *

At 5:35, the cyclone struck the upper Midwest, churning breezes into zephyrs and creating meteorological conditions that were conducive to starting fires and spreading them rapidly.

In towns like Oconto and Peshtigo on the western edge of Green Bay, and New Franken, and Rosiere east of the Bay, families were sitting down to a light Sunday supper just hours after the midday dinner. There was a bizarre stillness across the region, the literal calm before the storm, interrupted only by the sound of breezes that were building in intensity. It was the kind of evening that put everyone on edge.

Off in the distance, southwest of the lumber communities, the stillness in the vast green sea of pine trees was interrupted violently. Winds gained force. They fanned isolated small fires that had combusted in the dry brush. Gusts not only increased the size of the tiny blazes but pushed them along, so they could attack more brush, dead leaves, and moisture-less trees. Within minutes, the many minor fires began converging. Full scale forest fires were climbing tree trunks, cascading from tree to tree until a raging inferno was spreading acre after acre. Next, the firestorm fanned outward, becoming larger as it continued its irrevocable path to the northeast. Its speed accelerated. Its din became louder. Its heat became incendiary. Everything in its path was charred or reduced to ruins in a matter of seconds.

Below the town of Oconto, farmer Abraham Place had just finished securing his barn for the night. Horses, cows, pigs, and chickens were locked in. But the four horses were restless, no, more than that, they were agitated. They whined, pawed the floor of their stalls, and attempted to rear up but the ropes connecting their bridals to the wall kept them from rising completely. The cows shifted uncomfortably and seemed unable to settle for the night. The pigs snorted more than usual and the chickens ran around in their coop and would not go into their individual compartments. Abe Place recognized these signs and decided he would search for other signals when he left the barn.

Those signs came to him immediately as he left the structure. In the distance he could hear an ominous roaring noise. It was not a typical sound, not like the roar of a growing wind gust. It was more like the whoosh of a tornado or the roar of a giant waterfall as it crashed over the edge.

Before the awful sound could register fully, Abraham Place gazed toward the southwest. Smoke billowed skyward. Monster flames were shooting in every direction. He could feel a wave of hot, oppressive air taking dead aim at his property.

He stood frozen, his life rapidly replaying in his brain. He recalled the long, arduous journey from Northern Vermont to Northern Wisconsin in 1837, his decision to purchase eight hundred acres of pristine land, his marriage to an Indian woman and the five children borne of their love, his prosperity as a farmer, and his recent concerns about the drought and its possible impact on the family, his home and barn. He also reflected on his decision to plow circles around his structures with the help of his sons, to act as a fire barrier.

"Fire!' he yelled, snapping out of his reverie. Abe ran toward the house.

"Fire! I say," he repeated. "Fire!"

The front door of his house sprang open. His eldest son Isaac came to the edge of the front porch.

At a gallop, the father yelled once more.

"Fire coming from the southwest," he screamed, "we must take action to save the house."

Isaac turned back to the doorway.

"Abel, Nehemiah, girls, get the blankets," he ordered. "Mother, put the ladder against the house. Quickly. Everyone into action now."

Rosanna, their mother, was a strong, sturdy woman. She knew her responsibility for the rescue mission. The Place family had practiced its strategic plan for saving the property. All seven of them knew exactly what to do and they set about their jobs quickly.

Rosanna ran out the back door and to the side of the six-room wooden house. Grabbing the wooden ladder that was lying on the ground parallel to the building, she hoisted the ladder so that it leaned against the porch roof. Within moments, Abel, Nehemiah, and their sisters Esther and Elizabeth rushed into the front yard, armed to their chins with blankets.

Isaac meanwhile had run out the back door to the pond some fifty feet from the house. Remarkably, it had not dried up through the long dry spell. Abraham was convinced it was spring fed so that surface drought could not evaporate the pond's underground aquifer. Isaac carried four buckets. He and his brothers would fill the buckets, then run them to a pair of barrels at the end of the porch, adjacent to where the ladder now stood. The boys' mission was to fill the barrels with water.

Rosanna and the girls then took the blankets and doused them in the water. Abe hauled the moistened blankets up the ladder and begin laying them across the roof. Given their weight he could carry only two or three at a time, so he was required to make many trips up and down the ladder.

When the three boys finished the barrel-filling operation, they assisted the women. Isaac took wet blankets and scaled the ladder to assist his father in placing them atop the wooden shingles. The younger boys dampened blankets until the water level began to drop significantly in the barrels. Nehemiah and Abel each grabbed two pails and retreated to the water hole to refill their buckets and later the barrels.

When Abraham and Isaac had covered the front half of the house, they noticed three other men approaching the property from the road which meandered into Oconto. They were some of Rosanna's Indian relatives and were coming to help with the fireproofing.

"Two of you fetch water," Abe yelled from the rooftop, "and one help us carry blankets up here."

The newcomers sprang into action. With ten people engaged in the mission, it took about 30 minutes to cover the house and porch roof. But the job was only partially completed.

"It is coming closer," Abraham said to the group as he descended the ladder for the last time. "Now we must wet down the walls."

"Father, what about the barn," Isaac inquired.

"We have plowed the ground deeper there," his father replied. "We will have to trust that the barrier will stop the flames as they fall into the hole."

Abraham had always known that the house was the first priority to save. In addition to plowing around it, the family had made sure there were enough blankets to cover the top. The barn was too large for the blanket cover.

Next, the Place family members and helpers dipped their buckets into the barrels, extracted water, and proceeded to hurl it at the walls of the house. The idea was to throw the water toward the top of the wall, allowing the moisture to run down and coat the entire wall. As some of them wet the walls, others ran furiously to the pond to replenish the barrels. Around the four sides of the house they went. No one slowed, despite the muscle- and back-aches which were developing from the weight of the water buckets and the blankets. Then, Abraham directed the men to throw water on the side of the barn that faced the approaching fire. They scurried from pond, to barrels, to barn and back, trying desperately to beat the approaching blaze.

"Good God!" exclaimed Isaac. He had stopped just long enough to look toward the southwest, in an effort to chart the fire's progress. "Faster, everyone, faster."

The jobs were done but the task was not over.

"Rosanna, take the girls into the house for now and stay in the kitchen," Abe ordered. The kitchen was on the northeast side of the house, away from the initial brunt of the impending blaze. She herded Elizabeth and Esther into the house.

"When I tell you, throw water over your heads and faces," Abraham told her. "But wait until I say so."

The men were near the front porch, eyeing the fiery tornado as it barreled toward them, although it still appeared several miles off. The wind speed increased and with it came a loud, shrill sound that pierced the ears as it approached.

"It is time to re-wet the roof," Abe advised his helpers. "Abel, Nehemiah, run to the pond and re-fill the barrels. The boys did as directed. Abe, his son, and the Indians formed a chain. Abe went to the roof, followed quickly by Isaac. The other men positioned themselves strategically. One stood at the barrels. He would fill a bucket and hand it to a man at the bottom of the ladder, who passed it to the third man near the top of the ladder. Abe and Isaac rushed over, took the pails, then poured the water onto the blankets, which were drying from the heat of the day and the now-not-distant fire. With the roof re-wetting accomplished, all hands turned to the task of moistening the walls again. Then the men ran back to the barn to wet down its walls.

Despite intense and almost unbearable heat, a stiff wind, and approaching exhaustion, the men finished the tasks. Abe Place was convinced the more water that was used, the more likely the house would survive a fire.

The gathering inferno was now invading his property line, whipped furiously by hurricane-like winds.

"More water, men!" screamed Abraham, wanting every opportunity to cheat the fire of the chance to destroy his beloved home.

The roar of the fire was deafening. The heat became overwhelming. Flames shot several feet into the air. Sparks flew like fireworks, igniting new fires in the dense and dry brush and grass. The blaze galloped as fast as that of any of Abe's horses. It attacked part of his fence that surrounded one grazing field.

"Keep throwing water on the walls until I tell you to enter the house," Abraham barked above the din of the approaching inferno.

It was now less than one hundred feet from the house, a gaping yellow monster, howling, spitting, destroying almost everything in its path.

"God forgive me," prayed Abraham. "Spare us."

And then, a fateful event.

A crosswind.

It blew the massive blaze to the right, no longer taking direct aim at the Place house. Still, Abe thought, the fire could be unpredictable and the wind could change direction again. There was no more time to take protective action. The time for self-preservation had come.

"Everyone inside, now!" Abraham Place instructed his sons and relatives. They hustled into the kitchen where the women crouched by the sink near two pails of tepid water.

When all ten of them were together, Abe and Rosanna took cloths, immersed them in the water, and wiped the heads and faces of the others. The girls were treated first, then the boys, then Rosanna's kinfolk, then Abe and herself. Finally, they doused four blankets. They ordered groups to crouch together on the kitchen floor, then placed the wet blanket over each group. Even as they assumed this position, they could all feel the heat rising and smoke began pouring under the door, as well as through cracks in the windows and walls.

They waited, shivering from fear, not heat. And they prayed.

The great roar of the crosswind blew the fire away from the house. But because of its sheer size, it was still possible that embers from the inferno might strike the house. The wind was swirling, similar to a tornado. The fire raced across the open ground of the pasture and lost some of its ferocity. By missing the house, there was less kindling to enlarge the red, hot flames. Fortunately for Abraham Place and his extended family, the wind actually became an ally. As it blew the blaze away from the structure, it sent the fire toward a wooded area, which was what it wanted and needed to grow in size and strength.

Reaching the tree line, the fire raged anew. Flames and sparks jumped. Several landed on the roof of the house, only to fizzle on contact with the slightly-moist blankets. But there was a new danger. Part of the fire trailed off from the main inferno and ate its way through the dry grass toward the front of the home. But the wet walls of the house stopped the flames. The water did its job, preventing serious fire damage. Embers died, their color slowly changing from orange to a dull black. They were impotent, unable to set the house on fire.

The Place family waited through it all. Only when the sound of the fury lessened did the weary refugees remove the blankets and examine their immediate surroundings. All four blankets had been dried by the heat and smoke which accompanied the flames. They may have been utterly useless had the fire struck the house directly. But no one dwelled on that. They were consumed with gratitude that the house, barn, and all of them had been spared.

Slowly they moved from the kitchen, walking cautiously to the front door of the house, to inspect what damage had been done in the few minutes the fire had disrupted their lives.

Abraham was the first to notice the black path, as the fire had charged toward his home. He inspected the front, the side, and the back of the structure to assure himself nothing was burning, or threatened. He walked completely around the structure twice, marveling that it had been spared. There was some discoloration of the wood on the wall where the fire had struck a glancing blow but no further damage. He lifted the ladder again and scaled the rungs until he reached the roof. He saw the several burnished embers but knew they had done no serious damage to his roof.

Abe Place said a silent prayer of thanksgiving, then yelled down that the roof had survived. Down below him, he heard cheers from the men, while Rosanna and the girls held hands and danced around in a small circle, happy to be alive and safe and still have a home.

From his perch above the house, Abe Place watched the forest fire heading away from his property. As it gnawed its way through trees and brush, it became even more ferocious, more noisy, and more nasty. Abe Place could only stand and watch, in awe of its absolute power. And he could only think how devastating it would become as it gained momentum in the miles of forest land ahead of it.

*   *   *

Less than five miles away, the traveling inferno took dead aim at the property of John Church. He was a grain farmer who, like his neighbors, had watched in desperation as the protracted drought had all but ruined his crops. His two horses, used for transportation, had become thin and sickly because he did not have enough money to buy proper feed. The animals had always been able to eat grass in the fields, supplemented by straw and grain, and had remained fit. But now the grass was dry and inedible and John Church could not spare the money for horse fodder. He needed every cent to feed his wife Emma and his three growing boys. Ephraim, the eldest, was fifteen, John Junior was a year younger, and Terrence was the baby, at twelve.

The family had just finished dinner and dishes when a distant rumbling sound unnerved John. He ran from the house. In the waning light of that October day, he scanned the sky. He stood motionless, transfixed. To the southwest he detected what, at first, appeared to be a brilliant sunset. Then he noticed the flames, the accompanying roar, the clouds of smoke, the advancing heat. He ran back to the home's front, where he was met by the rest of the family, staring in utter disbelief and sheer terror.

"What shall we do?" cried Emma Church. "Should be run?"

"No," her husband shouted, "we must try to protect the house and barn. It is all we have."

"John, I would rather have nothing and save my life than be caught in that fire," said Emma.

"I think we can protect the property from the flames and save ourselves," John retorted.

The three boys said nothing, listening intently to their parents' argument.

Peshtigo

"Everyone get a bucket," John ordered. "We must wet down the house and barn so the fire will not burn them."

The boys sprang into action, grabbing pails, dipping them in two barrels of water, and heaving the water at the house. They all worked at the same pace. After moistening each side of the house thoroughly, they moved to the next side.

John and Emma took on the responsibility of trying to protect the barn.

They worked without talking because the din from the wind and flames was now so loud, none of the Church family members could hear anything above the roar.

Ephraim, young John and Terrence threw water on each side of the house twice. Then the oldest son instructed his brothers to join him at the barn to help his parents there. As he ran from one structure to the second, Terrence cast a glance at the approaching fire. It was so big, so hot, so loud, he found himself trembling.

With five people on the detail, the water storage barrels near the barn ran low.

"Ephraim, John," their father shouted, "run to the barrels nearest the house and bring water back in the buckets. We need more to coat the barn." John Church now began to cough. Raising his voice, breathing in advancing smoke, and the strenuous activity, had combined to clog his throat and fill his lungs. He had to stop his rescue activity momentarily until he could clear his throat and cough his lungs free of the foul air. He bent over the water container, cupped his hands and took a drink.

"John, hurry, the fire is so close," Emma screamed.

She had barely finished her plea when the inferno tore across the field, in a blistering blaze of flame and heat so intense it knocked Emma to the ground. John ran to help her but before they could move, the fire roared over them and attacked the barn. Even though the Church family had doused it, the structure's dry wood provided even more strength to the fire, sending flames heaving a hundred feet into the air, casting flying sparks in all directions, incinerating the building, melting its concrete floor, and obliterating the stalls. The horses were burned to death before they could move.

Emma screamed fiercely as the flames surrounded her.

"Help me! Help me! Help!!" screamed John Church. Then he was silent.

Terrence, at the back of the barn, saw the firestorm lunge at the building. He turned and ran from the force of the inferno. He headed to the stream several hundred yards from the house. He did not hear nor did he see his parents as they burned to death.

The voracious fire now targeted the Church house as its next victim. It moved so fast it mowed down the two older boys as they were trying to escape.

Their screams of horror lasted only a few seconds.

The inferno marched on, leaving in its wake a pile of ash and cinder several inches high. Within minutes, the barn and house were decimated. All that remained standing was the fireplace and some metal fragments, twisted and scarred. Not a single part of the Church residence was recognizable, save the chimney. Nearby, the well-water pump, which had not been used in weeks because the well had gone dry, had disappeared. Pieces of the pump fell down into the well hole.

The fire, now more like a tornado, was moving northwest at a furious pace. And left behind, crouched and crying in the stream at the Church property's edge, Terrence raised himself out of the chilly water. He first feared the fire might make its way to the stream, after ripping through the barn and house but the monster had gone away from it. The water was cold but it was his lifeline. Terrence did not move. He could not move. He was scared but he was also angry with himself. He had abandoned the others to save himself. He had no idea what had happened to his parents or to his two brothers. He hoped that his mother and father had decided at the last minute to sprint to safety and that his older brothers had made the same decision.

The drone of the fire had dissipated, the incredible heat had dissolved, the bright flames had moved on. As he stood to survey his family ground, Terrence Church could see little as the brightness from the fire was replaced by darkness.

Gathering his courage and strength, Terrence trudged up the incline from the creek toward the house. He knew the barn had burned but he was not certain about the fate of the family house. The darkness deepened and he realized he was shivering, now that the fire's immense heat had moved on. He was soaked through from his time in the water and the cooling temperature made him uncomfortable. His touched his face and discovered it was caked with mud, his eyes were sore from crying. His shoes sloshed as he walked, filled with spring water. After a few minutes, he decided to call out.

"Mother, Father, Ephraim, John, can you hear me?"
Nothing.
"Where are you?"
No reply.

His shivers now combined with fearful trembling. He heard no sounds from his family and no cries from the horses. Then he stumbled into the rubble. As he took a few more steps, Terrence could make out the chimney.

"Good Lord," he blurted out loud. The house is destroyed, he told himself. He looked in the direction of the barn but could see no structure. He walked toward it, then reached a mound of ash.

"Our barn," he whispered, "and there is nothing left of it."
"Ephraim, John, can you hear me?"
"Father, Mother, where are you?"

The quiet was even more unsettling now than the explosive sound of the fire had been. Terrence became very frightened. He could not find his family. His home was destroyed, so he had no place to shelter and no opportunity to change into some dry clothes. His shivers became almost uncontrollable. And they competed with his sobs.

"What am I going to do?" he asked out loud. There was no response. There was no sound at all.

The twelve-year-old stumbled toward what he knew was a large maple tree that stood near the house. He thought he would sit against the tree and wait for his family to return. But as he walked he realized he had gone too far. He turned back and strained his eyes. The tree was not there. Gone, just like the house.

Now the tears came, in torrents. The boy felt alone, abandoned, afraid. He did not know what to do or where to go. The nearest neighbor was a few miles away. He had never made the journey in the dead of night. He groped his way back toward what was his home. As he approached the ashes, he discovered they were still warm. He sat near the pile in an effort to warm himself against the wet of his clothes and the chill of the night. And there he sat, overcome with fear. He did not move for many minutes, his emotions overwhelming him.

Finally, the shock and stress of the past few hours took their toll. Terrence Church fell into a type of sleep. Indeed, he fell over from his sitting position and he lay near the still-smoldering embers. He remained there all through the night.

*   *   *

There was not just one fire, but many. A broad band of blazes broke out, spread, and kindled new fires all along the western edge of the Green Bay. They extended several miles in length and width. The winds energized them all and kept them moving, which allowed the fires to destroy all that stood in their way. One band of fires started several miles west of Oconto but they ultimately converged into one firestorm, massive in size and intensity. It was worse than the biggest blast furnace imaginable. Flames shot hundreds of feet into the night sky. Visibility improved for miles around the storm because its flames were so bright. The noise was deafening, louder than a train. The pressure from the center of the fires was so strong it launched trees like rockets into the air. When they returned to earth, flames and sparks shattered in every direction, lighting more trees, bushes, and brush. The fires moved unusually fast. They fed off each other and gained a terrible and swift momentum.

Animals raced for cover but many could not outrun the inferno. Some dug deep into the ground but to no avail because the fire was so intense, it burned down into the ground as well as up into the sky. Other creatures were crushed by falling trees and limbs. Many birds were able to fly away from danger but others were sucked into the fire's vengeance and incinerated.

The tidal wave of flame and smoke now danced across the Oconto River, deep in the western woods. Its unimaginable force was now marching irrevocably toward the three isolated Sugar Bush communities. For many families, nighttime activities indoors kept them from noticing the approach of the killer fire. Only a few folks saw it coming. They were more fortunate than the rest.

Peshtigo

Alfred and Mildred Phillips were sitting in their plushly-decorated log cabin, reading by candle light and oil lamp. He was midway through the Charles Dickens' novel *David Copperfield*.

She was immersed in a New Testament chapter of the Bible. The couple had enjoyed a light supper just an hour before, then had worked together to wash and put away the dishes. Their Sunday nights were often spent this way, either reading or in quiet conversation. At the end of their normally-busy week, Sunday was spent relaxing, right up until bedtime.

At first it started as a dull rumbling sound, far off in the distance. Neither husband nor wife took much notice. But as the sullen sound became more clear, it unnerved the Phillips.

"Do you hear that?" Alfred asked his wife, looking up from his book.

"Why, yes," she replied, "it sounds like a train approaching but, of course, we have no train as yet."

"How odd because it sounds to me like ocean waves coming in to pound against the shore but, of course, we are nowhere near the ocean."

They dismissed the sound and returned to their reading.

But the outside roar persisted, propelling the conflagration northward on its devastating path.

The Phillips' house was furnished grandly and that included window coverings. Mildred had ordered expensive thick drapes for the sitting room windows. In normal winters, they were excellent at rebuffing icy blasts of cold air but they were generally tied back for summer. Now in the autumn, although temperatures remained well above normal from the drought, Mildred had decided it was time to close the curtains for the year. The thick fabric acted as a form of insulation from the heat but it also muffled the sound of the approaching wildfire.

It was now about a mile wide and stretched several miles in length. And still it grew bigger. Once the brushfire reached the acres of open fields owned by Alfred Phillips, its pace was slowed somewhat but the violent wind kept forcing it onward.

Alfred Phillips looked up again. He now thought he heard a sound coming from the opposite direction. He lay his book on his lap and listened. It was just the wind, he concluded, and went back to *David Copperfield* once more.

It took just a few more seconds. The train-ocean sound became extraordinary, almost deafening. It startled both of them. They looked at each other and fear filled their eyes. Alfred jumped from his chair and shuffled to the front door. As he opened it a force of infrared air raced past him into the house. The fire was about to lunge at the cabin.

Alfred had no time to take action, no time even to turn and call to his wife.

The blaze literally leapt at the house. The wind created by the firestorm was so strong it nudged the house from its foundation, even as the conflagration burned the building and its contents.

But now a second current of wind, the other sound Alfred Phillips had heard, blew back against the fire with equal force. The cross-currents created a fiery tornado, swirling violently, with the Phillips' small house caught in the middle. The winds lifted the house from the ground, igniting it as it was carried higher. The six-room cabin was launched some one hundred feet into the air, all the while swirling and swerving like a children's top.

When it reached its apex, the home burst into flames and exploded, with fragments flung hundreds of feet in all directions. Bits of wood, brick, metal, and fabric blew in circles for several minutes until the fire passed completely and the objects could drift back to the scorched earth.

Alfred Phillips had been thrown back into the parlor after opening the front door. He fell down on his back. As the home began to gyrate, he was hurled against a wall, hitting his head, knocking him out. Mildred Phillips had been so stunned and then so frightened by the fire's assault, she never moved from her chair. Both died when the house exploded. It took just two minutes from the time Alfred opened the door until the house particles rained back down to the ground.

*   *   *

All three of the Sugar Bush communities were under a smoky siege.

Peshtigo

Charles Lamp considered himself fortunate. He had seen the fire's approach in the distance and took immediate action. He could tell from the sheer size of the inferno that there was no time to try to save his home or barn. All he could do was organize an evacuation to save his family and himself. He sprinted into the house and sounded the alarm.

"Nellie!" he shouted. "Get the children, get coats on quickly, and gather near the front steps. There is a fire coming. I will team the horses on the wagon and we will try to outrun it. Hurry!"

As Nellie ran to fetch Joseph, Mary, and Carl, Charles Lamp raced to the barn, tore open the doors, dragged the wagon out into the open, and pulled the two horses out of their stalls and into position at the front of the wagon.

His task was made more difficult by the smoke and wind that was bringing the blaze ever closer. The haze lodged in Charles' throat and he began coughing uncontrollably. The sight and sound of the impending fire terrified the horses. They were unwilling to be drawn any closer to the inferno. Even when he had hitched them to the wagon, it was nearly impossible to keep them under control. Both beasts wanted to run as far and as fast as they could. Charles managed to get into the buckboard and forced the horses from the barn to the front porch of the house, where Nellie and the children were waiting. All were wearing their coats and hats; Nellie had even brought a coat and hat for her husband.

While Charles held the reins tightly so the horses would not move, Nellie helped each child on board. All of them huddled together just behind the wagon's seat. As Nellie jumped aboard, the fire was just yards away.

Charles forced the horses into action and they sped off around the house, trying to escape the clutches of the flames. But the firestorm, with wind gusts sounding like unending thunder claps, roared quickly past the Lamp house and in the direction of the fleeing wagon.

Charles had managed to reach the main dirt road that ran from Lower Sugar Bush, north to Middle and Upper Sugar Bush. He was fortunate because the fire had not reached the road itself but it was charging through the forested areas off to the side.

The Lamp family gazed in awe and terror at the mammoth blaze as it rushed past them, but several feet away. Charles was amazed at the speed of the fire, the height of the flames, the sparks that shot into the air like flares, and the all-consuming heat. He was glad he had not put on his coat. He was perspiring madly now from fear and exertion. He could only assume the heat made his coat-clad wife and children painfully uncomfortable.

Charles had his eyes on the horses, making sure he could keep them on the road. Although darkness had fallen, the path was easy to see because of the fervent brightness of the flames.

"Charles," he wife yelled through the din, "the fire is coming closer to the road."

He hadn't noticed that the wind had swerved slightly and that the blaze was moving toward the dirt road. Now he played a mental game with himself. Should he risk stopping the team and letting the fire pass in front of his family and then perhaps blow away from them. Or might the changing wind blow the inferno back in their direction. He knew if that happened, he would not have time to turn the team and the wagon around to flee. His other option was to press the horses harder, try to make them gallop faster, try to outrun the fire.

He chose that option, yelling at his team to pick up the pace.

But the fire moved faster than the team. Charles Lamp was taking his family and his horses into a fiery trap, from which there seemed little chance of escape. The blaze edged closer to the road now, the thunder of the wind punctuated by popping sounds, as the fire engulfed trees and the heat made them explode. It was all too much for the children. They began to scream and call for their mother. Nellie turned and tried to comfort them but knew she would not be able to go to them given the speed at which the wagon was traveling.

Without warning, a fire-ravaged tree fell directly across the roadway. The inferno followed it across the road, setting the opposite side ablaze. The wagon was about to be surrounded.

Charles pulled feverishly on the reigns to stop the horses before they careened into the blazing branches. But even this success was short-lived because the ocean of fire was now rolling directly toward the Lamp family wagon. Charles jumped from the wagon, trying to

Peshtigo

push the horses back from the downed tree, then attempting to turn them around in the other direction. But it was too late.

The fire bore down from two sides and consumed the wagon.

"Aaagh!" screamed a terrified Nellie. The cries of the children became louder.

Just a few feet away but unscathed, Charles panicked. Instead of trying to help his family, he ran. To his utter amazement, he noticed a stream about thirty feet away from the road. He lunged into the water and covered himself against the intense fire but as he came up for air every few seconds, he could still feel the unbearable heat. After about twenty dunkings, he noticed the heat level seemed lower. He looked around him. The fire had passed. It had taken its light with it. Darkness surrounded him.

Charles Lamp's automatic reaction for survival had been so strong, he had ignored his family's fate. Now, as he stood in the center of the stream, a wave of guilt washed over him. He ran to the wagon, still smoldering on the road. He approached it slowly, and discovered it had been incinerated completely. Thick black-gray ashes where once a wooden wagon had been.

He kicked through the debris with his boot, eventually touching something hard. Some type of metal. He peered into the faint light of the embers, surrounded by ominous darkness. It was the metal that had covered one of the wagon wheels. Then he found another. A few feet away, another charred piece of iron. One of the horses' bits. And then, a blackened piece of wool. Part of his wife's coat. Finally, the most frightening find of all. A burned bit of bone beneath the coat fabric.

Charles Lamp broke down in tears. His escape had saved himself but it had left his wife, his children, and two horses to face a horrible death.

* * *

For Henry Bateman, it was the end of another evening's milking. On this Sunday night, he had help with the twenty cows waiting for attention. Henry's ten-year-old son Joshua did a few and a neighbor boy, Edward Bartell, pitched in as well. He was twelve years old and he was the oldest of Henry Bartell's eight children.

Elizabeth Bateman was there too because she knew the heat and haze of the day would make the chore even harder than normal.

It had been a major subject of conversation in Lower Sugar Bush. Dairy farmer Henry Bateman lived next to grain farmer Henry Bartell. The locals always addressed each man by his complete name because they had the same first name.

Henry and Elizabeth Bateman were doing Henry Bartell a favor. A widower, Henry Bartell had to travel to the state capital, Madison, to conduct some business. He told the Batemans he would be gone for about four days and wondered whether they might look after his brood of eight.

Now for some people, minding so many children might be an unthinkable task. But for Elizabeth Bateman, it was just a few more mouths to feed. And Henry Bartell had given her extra foodstuffs to feed his throng.

The Batemans decided it would be better if the Bartell children stayed with them in their home, so Henry Bartell marched his small army to the Bateman house before he set off for Madison.

He reintroduced each of the youngsters to his neighbors. Edward was twelve, twins Peter and Paul were eleven. Luke was nine, Eliza was a year younger. Then came Mark, aged seven, Lila who was five, and little Veronica was four.

The Bateman household was now brimming with two adults and fourteen children. But everyone seemed to fit in without much fuss. The four Bateman boys shared their sleeping space with the five Bartell boys. And the two Bateman daughters made room for the three Bartell sisters.

Sunday afternoon's dinner had looked more like a church supper, with sixteen adults and children reaching for food. Henry had put together two tables in the parlor to accommodate everyone. Elizabeth found it was no more stressful on her. She just doubled her recipes and served meals that were easy to make for crowds. And she liked the fact that, with so many hands in the house, she did not have to clean up after meals.

It was the end of the second day of the Bartell visit. Henry Bartell would be returning on Tuesday, if all went as planned.

In the early evening, Henry Bateman and his assistants headed to the barn for the day's second milking. Alone, it would take Henry as long as two hours, tightening his arm muscles after milking twenty animals. When his wife and one or more of the children helped, it could cut the time in half. Despite the offers to help, however, the youngsters sometimes made more work for Henry and the task could take two hours or more. But on this particular day, the two boys worked efficiently and effectively, so the milking and storing activity took slightly more than an hour. A wagon would come tomorrow to collect most of the milk and carry it to a dairy in Marinette for processing. The rest would be used for the Bateman clan.

Henry and the boys were looking forward to a light Sunday supper. But after putting the milk up for storage, and leaving the barn, the sight that greeted them put any thought of eating out of their minds.

Henry could not believe his eyes, when he first caught sight of the smoke rising above the tree tops. Then, flames shot up above the trees and jumped quickly to other trees, setting them alight. Henry was now also aware of a powerful breeze that stoked the wildfire. He stood still for a moment to gauge its direction and then realized to his horror that it was coming directly toward his barn from the southwest.

"Boys, come quickly," he said, and his apprentice milkers ran after him to the house.

Entering the house, he announced to his wife, "There is a big fire coming this way, so gather up all the children."

Elizabeth removed some pans from the heat of the stove and was on the move immediately, retrieving the several small children, scattered about the Bateman house. While she was on her rescue mission, Henry returned to the front of the house, trying to assess the size of this approaching wall of fire and what his options were. From what he could see, the huge blaze was on a path directly toward his barn. Without hesitating, he ran to the building, opened the doors and released the cows. He grabbed a switch and forced the frightened animals out into an open pasture adjacent to the barn. Henry calculated that if the cows remained in the barn, they were likely to be killed by flames with no chance of escape. But if he allowed them to run freely, they might be more fortunate and actually survive. Chances of that seemed slim in either case but he felt he must give the cows every opportunity to protect themselves and preserve their lives.

Henry next ran back to the house. Elizabeth had assembled all fourteen children in one place. Her parlor looked like an overcrowded classroom.

Before entering his wooden home, Henry turned again to chart the course of the fire. It still appeared to be aiming at the barn and that side of the property. He was not certain whether it would avoid the house; it seemed to grow bigger and become more powerful as flames gobbled up more trees and brush. But he didn't dare let everyone remain in the house because if the blaze veered toward it, everyone inside would be incinerated.

Time was running out.

"Follow me and Mrs. Bateman out into the pasture," he commanded. "When we get to a certain place, lie down on your stomachs, take your hands and loosen some dirt, and put your face right down in the dirt."

He marched off, Elizabeth followed, then a swarm of young people ran after them. They charged through the opened pasture gate. They noted that many of the cows were running away from the house and barn, apparently devising their own plans of escape.

When he reached the farthest corner of the field, he stopped. He told them to lie down, five abreast, and start turning the soil with their hands. Most of them understood but Henry had to help Lila and Veronica Bartell and Elizabeth decided to loosen the earth for her baby child, two-year-old Raymond.

After turning over the soil for the girls and looking up, Henry liked and disliked what he saw. The wind seemed to be blowing the blaze away from them and toward the barn. But, as it gusted, it shifted the fire's direction. It also enlarged and spread the fire. Henry concluded there was no place else to go, so his family and visiting-family would have to take their chances in the open field.

The heat of the inferno now blew out from the core and spread over them. The younger children began sobbing, fearing the heat would harm them. Coupled with the growing din of the swirling wind, the brushfire frightened all of them. But Henry took comfort in watching the fire blow away from where they lay.

Peshtigo

"Please God, keep it on that path," Henry prayed, partially to himself.

His wife, lying next to him, heard his plea.

"Amen!" she said.

"Here it comes," Henry shouted to the rest. "Everyone down, bury your faces in the dirt so they won't get burned by the heat, put your hands under your body so they are not burned. And say a prayer."

It approached with a freight train roar, the wind blowing the loose dirt around their heads and faces. The temperature rose. Just breathing in the heat-warmed environment became difficult.

With one climactic howl, the fiery train passed them by but took several minutes for it to leave completely. No one moved.

There was a giant smashing sound. Henry Bateman looked up. The barn was fully engulfed in flame. The roof and walls were crashing inward to the floor. Then there was a loud explosion as the pressure from the heat and flames reached the wood, straw, tools, and milking equipment in the ravaged building. Henry could take no more of it. He dropped his head to the ground, whimpering quietly as his loss.

When the oppressive heat, flames, and smoke had passed and the wind became a distant but persistent din, Henry looked up again. This time he was joined by his wife.

"Our barn is in ruins," he said, "but the house was untouched."

"Best of all," she responded, "we have survived, every last one of us. God has been good to us."

"Children, you can move now," Henry told the little ones.

Many of their faces were reddened, as if the children had taken too much sun on a hot summer day. Faces and hands were also covered with flecks of dirt. Elizabeth inspected each of them.

"There is some burning but I have some lotion in the house to treat it," she said.

"We have been very fortunate," Henry Bateman said to all of them. "Our house appears undamaged, even though the barn is gone. Let us go inside and rest."

It was dusk now, with the light fast fading, but the smoke and haze left behind by the blaze made visibility even more difficult. Henry led the crowd back through the pasture toward the house. As they marched, he could hear the odd cow moo-ing in the distance. He was comforted to realize that at least some of his flock survived the onslaught. In the morning, he would assess the damage to his barn, his property, and his animals.

When all sixteen of them were in the parlor and candles had been lit, Henry asked for everyone's attention.

"If the fire does not return we will go out early tomorrow to assess the damage. I will take some of you boys with me. We also need to search for our cows. I let them out of the barn. Some must have survived because I heard them tonight. God was with us and brought us through this ordeal."

Henry knelt down in the middle of the parlor floor. Everyone else followed his lead. He led them in a prayer of thanksgiving for their deliverance from danger.

*   *   *

The Newtons of the Upper Sugar Bush settlement were a close family. Adnah Newton was the patriarch of a family which extended over two adjacent farms. He lived with his wife Margaret, her aging mother Florence, and an adopted orphan called Tess. Adnah and Margaret had taken her in, even though they were middle-aged.

In the neighboring farm, son Samuel lived with his wife Anna and their two young children, five-year old Peter, and his sister Mary who was three.

The three generations lived in happiness and harmony on their land. They farmed together, often dined together, played together, and worshiped as a group each Sunday. Life was good.

They also prayed together at home, asking God for rain, for cooler temperatures, and for salvation from the unfortunate conditions that had persisted for months.

So far, those prayers remained unanswered. The elder Newton and his son were sitting on Adnah's porch as the sun disappeared behind a sea of pine trees. Dusk settled over the land as the temperature began to cool. But after several minutes, the two men noticed a brightening in the southwestern sky. The temperature rose and a breeze built steadily.

"Good Lord, son, is that fire moving this way?"

Peshtigo

"I think it is and it is a big one!" responded Sam.

"Round up all the family while I think about what to do."

It was fortunate for everyone that both families were in Adnah's house. They had all gathered for Sunday dinner after church and remained for the afternoon and early evening. The three adult women - Florence, her daughter Margaret, and Sam's wife Anna - had spent the evening talking and working on a quilt, to which they were all contributing. The three children had been amusing themselves in various ways both inside and outside the house. At the moment they were in the Tess' room playing with wooden building blocks.

Samuel stormed through the front door, frightening the women as they quilted in the sitting room.

"Anna, please run and get the children," he said as calmly as he could. "Bring them here quickly. There is a great fire and we think it is moving toward us so we must do something."

Sam's wife dropped her needle and ran to the bedroom to fetch the children.

"We will just wait here until Anna and the young 'uns come back," Sam said. "Pa is trying to decide what is best for us to do."

Florence and Margaret rushed to the door to look for the fire that had been reported to them.

"Oh my word!" gasped the elderly woman, "I have never seen a fire such as that."

Margaret seemed equally astonished, asking of Samuel, "Son, what will we do?"

"Pa will think of a plan," Sam said, "he will come in shortly and tell us."

Sam's wife hustled Tess, Peter, and Mary into the front room and all awaited the family patriarch.

The fire ranged closer and it seemed to grow larger and more intense. The ground rumbled as the inferno advanced. The younger children became frightened. Tess, who was older, was uneasy.

"Now children," Sam knelt on one knee near Mary and Peter, "there is a big fire coming this way but Grampa will make sure everything is all right. We must do everything he says." Tess nodded silently, indicating she too understood.

At that moment, Adnah came to the porch with two shovels and some burlap bags, the kind used to ship potatoes or animal feed.

He entered the sitting room and addressed his extended family.

"There is no place to hide in the house or barn. And because our pond and well are nearly dry, there is no way to water down the buildings. We must leave them to their fate. We cannot outrun this fire so we will get out in the open away from wooded areas."

"But Adnah, a fire that big will burn us no matter where we stand," said his wife.

"That may be true but we will get below ground, in the sandy area near the pig pen," he responded. "Samuel and I will dig trenches and we will all get in them. I will cover each of you with a sack, then put sand on top of that. With luck, the fire will pass over us with little harm."

"Is there enough time?" asked Adnah's wife Margaret.

"Who knows?" Sam replied, "but we must hurry!" He ushered everyone out the door toward the pig sty.

The wind was stronger now and they had trouble seeing as sand and dust were being blown furiously into their eyes, noses, and mouths. When they reached the pig pen, it was deserted. There were no hogs there now. As the drought lingered and feed dried up, Adnah decided months ago to take them to Green Bay for slaughter while he could still sell them. Fortunately, he had cleaned the pen after the sale.

Adnah pulled his wife and mother-in-law into the sandy section of the sty. Samuel helped Anna escort the three children. When all had arrived, the women and children turned their backs to the wind and tried to shield their faces from the heat of the approaching blaze.

The two men set to work, shoveling furiously. Because the sand was so dry, it was easy to dig and they excavated a long, deep hole in a matter of minutes that would accommodate all eight of them. Adnah threw several burlap sacks down on the pit floor so they could lie on them. Then he told Anna to make the children lie down in the middle of the hole. The women went to either side of them. Samuel covered them with another burlap bag. Then the men began hoisting sand on top of the women and children.

"We will not cover your heads because you will need to breathe," Adnah told them. "But when the fire gets close, we must hold our breath and cover our heads until it passes."

The women were skeptical, the children were terrified.

Adnah next ordered his son to lie at one end of the pit, near Anna. He dropped a cloth over Sam and poured sand over him. Then he turned to look at the impending inferno.

To his shock he saw flames already attacking trees at the edge of his property. Flames scurried up the trunks, licking at dead leaves and dry branches. When a tree had been weakened by the onslaught, it would tumble to the ground in a shower of sparks and embers. These in turn would ignite dry grass, brush, and bushes and the fire would grow wider. There was an incessant wind but Adnah also realized the firestorm produced an updraft and a side-draft. It forced flames to leap from tree to tree. Adnah thought he saw two fires, one on the ground and one in the tree tops. But he also saw something that made his skin crawl.

As trees toppled and burned, their stumps continued to burn as well. It seemed to Adnah that the fire not only went up the trees and along the ground but also burrowed deep down into the ground, destroying tree roots. If the fire went underground near the pig pit, Adnah surmised that he and his family would be baked to death.

"Please God, let us live," he prayed.

Then he knelt in the pit next to his wife and pulled some sand over his lower torso. He lay prostrate in the sand, and scooped other sand over the rest of him.

"All we can do now is wait and pray for a miracle," he shouted to his family above the roar of the fire. "But be listening for when I tell you to bury your heads. It will not be long now."

The conflagration rampaged along at a steady clip, its orange-hot flames devouring and devastating everything in its path. When it was just several feet from the Newton family, the patriarch gave the order.

"Bury your heads as deep as you can and hold your breath as long as you can."

The heat was so overwhelming it formed blisters on Adnah's forehead and cheeks.

The fire danced right over them, moving at about eight miles per hour. Given its size, Samuel thought it would never end. They all felt the intense heat, they heard the booming sound of the wind. The adults wanted to exhale and take another breath but they held out as long as they could. The children were too frightened to scream and they could not breathe even if they wanted to.

And then, it was gone.

There was silence.

One by one, the Newtons emerged from their sandy salvation. They said nothing at first.

"The Lord has answered our most recent prayers," said Adnah. "He has performed a miracle in our lives, even if we have no rain."

The children's hair was singed when the flames passed over them. They were burned or blistered on their faces, necks, backs and legs. But they were unscathed beyond that.

As they looked behind them, they saw what the fire had done. Adnah's barn was reduced to rubble. The house too was a heap of smoking ash. Samuel would soon discover his property had been obliterated as well.

The family members were disheartened. But they were alive and very grateful.

*   *   *

As the conflagration raced from south to north, Upper Sugar Bush was the last of the three connected towns affected.

Terrence Kelly continued to live on edge, worrying about smoke, rising temperatures, and the dry ground which he said could go up in flames almost instantaneously.

But Sundays were days of rest for Terrence and his family. His wife Penelope generally cooked only one meal, the mid-day supper. She and Terrence then washed the dishes and relaxed through the afternoon and evening hours.

As they sat in the parlor quietly, she mending socks and he reading the newspaper, they noticed an increase in the wind, which banged the front screen door against the door jam. At length, Terrence rose from his chair to close the main door.

"Oh no!"

Peshtigo

"Terrence, what is the matter?" inquired Penelope, with a touch of nervousness in her voice.

"There is a great fire over yonder and it is coming this way."

She sprang from her rocker and ran to the door.

"Good Lord, it *is* coming toward us. I will get the children."

"Get the girls," Terrence told her. "I will get the boys."

By the time each parent had gathered the children together in the parlor, the fire had moved quickly and was now even closer to the house.

The six of them moved out onto the front porch.

"What shall we do, Terrence?" asked his wife.

There was no reply.

"Terrence," she repeated, the fire blowing dangerously close.

"Daddy!" cried Charlotte.

Without a word, Terrence grabbed Malachy and began running.

"Terrence, where are you going?" his wife screamed after him. "What are we going to do?"

Terrence still said nothing. He was panicking, thinking he could save himself and the child nearest him by outrunning the fire.

"Dad, tell me where we are going and what is to become of Mother and the others?"

Terrence was confused, disoriented, frightened. In his haste to escape the fire, he was running directly toward it and the wails of his son made no impression on him.

Sensing impending doom if she did not act decisively, Penelope grabbed the infant Molly and began racing away from the fire and toward the town center.

"Children, follow me!" she commanded.

Aubrey took Charlotte's hand and tried to pull her along.

The baby was crying, uncomfortable by the rapid movement and sensing her mother's fears.

Charlotte began to cry and was reluctant to run along with her mother and brother, Aubrey. He continued yanking on her arm but she resisted. At one point she stopped.

"I am scared, Aubrey," she blurted out.

"So am I," he said, "but we have to run away from the fire. Come on."

He turned to start running again but he'd lost sight of his mother and baby sister.

"Mother, where are you? Mother!"

She had run on ahead as the fire, with its overwhelming heat and smoke, had barreled toward town. She assumed the children were right behind her. As the haze thickened, she began to cough, as much from the running as from the smoky mass that was now surrounding her. She stopped running and turned. But Aubrey and Charlotte were not behind her.

"Aubrey! Charlotte!" she part-screamed, part-coughed. "Children, where are you?"

All she could hear was the furious sound of the wind, swirling like a summer tornado, whipping smoke and flames closer.

She had no choice. She had to protect herself and her baby. She veered off between some houses and ran to the town pond, which she knew still had water in it. Swimming season was over but a swim now might just save her life.

"My God," she said as she scampered to the water hole, "help my babies and my husband and protect us from this fury. Amen."

She reached the pond and ran into the water. The heat from the fire made the chill of the water less intense. Penelope heard voices. Others from Upper Sugar Bush had decided to take the same course of action. They too had made a dash for the water.

"May we be safe," she prayed. Then she waited, and watched, as the huge collection of flames blew through the town, coming closer and closer to the pond.

* * *

C.R. Towsley was preparing for bed, even though it was early on this Sunday night in Oconto. He would rise early in the morning and head to Peshtigo to begin the plaster work on the Catholic church. Father Pernin had been away today but was likely to be there in the morning to assist in any way he could.

Annabelle Towsley was already in bed, reading through the latest issue of the local newspaper. It told of growing and spreading wildfires in the forest lands west of Oconto. It gave her a chill, even on such a warm October evening.

Peshtigo

"What is it, my love?" C.R. said as he joined her in bed, noticing her shiver.

"More fires out in the forests," she responded. "It worries me that they are increasing and the weather does not improve."

"It is so hot, I feel certain it will make rain clouds form and bring us some relief," her husband said hopefully. "I heard the wind picking up, so it may bring rain yet."

The Towsleys had spent a quiet day at home. As Father Pernin had canceled the Mass because of the construction at the church, the family decided to take it easy. C.R., Annabelle, and the four children slept later than usual, then had fresh eggs, home-made bread, and coffee for breakfast. While Jonathan and Bradford cleaned and stacked the breakfast dishes, daughters Mayme and Colleen helped their mother prepare the Sunday dinner. Today they would have ham, potatoes, and squash. Annabelle had bought a few apples at the store, although they were scarce this year because of the weather. She decided to make a pie.

The weather was so warm by early afternoon, C.R. moved a table and chairs out behind the house so they could enjoy a Sunday picnic. The meal had been splendid and after the clean-up, the family spent the afternoon quietly. The women knitted, sewed, or read. The men played horseshoes, after which C.R. took his youngest child, Colleen, for a run around the yard on his shoulders. It was something she had loved since early childhood and even though she was getting bigger, he was still able to carry her easily on his brawny back. The "Pappa-back ride", as she called it, cheered her. Colleen had been melancholy of late. She had recurring dreams about the fire. C.R. and Annabelle were doing all they could to try to dispel the fears from their daughter's mind. This piggyback ride was another small offering.

As the day drew down and the family retreated to the house, Jonathan commented on the current weather conditions.

"The heat seems to have increased the smoke," he said. "I wonder if there are more fires out there in the woods."

"I have not read the paper yet but the headline suggests there are fires farther out in the forests," his mother said.

"Well, a breeze is coming up," said C.R., "so it could be blowing in smoke from miles away."

They knew they could do nothing about it, so they entered the house, closed the door tight to seal out the smokey haze, and sat around the parlor in conversation.

After which, Annabelle went to the kitchen where she sliced some of the remaining loaf for each family member. She brewed some fresh coffee. Their light supper consisted of bread, a bit of butter, and the steaming coffee. It was generally all anyone wanted after their large lunch.

C.R. reminded the rest of his clan that he would be awakening early, then riding off to Peshtigo for the start of the plaster work.

"So your mother and I are turning in early," he informed the children.

They, in turn, said they would retire to their rooms early as well. It would be a chance to get some rest before a week of work and school and chores.

Now in bed, Annabelle continued reading the local journal while her husband tried to drift off to sleep. But he noticed the wind was increasing.

"See, I told you," he mumbled to his wife, "that wind just might bring some rain."

The sound was muffled somewhat because all three bedrooms were at the rear of the house, away from the approaching wind. Their location also prevented any of the Towsleys from seeing the horizon, which now became crimson, as a wall of fire pushed its way to their house.

The speed of the wind continued to increase, approaching gale force. It whisked the flames across the ground and through the trees. Then the wind blew bolts of flame up the tree trunks, the fire skipped across several acres of cleared land and ignited other sections of forest. The gusts of wind were like a hundred blast furnaces, pushing heat that was severe enough to burn skin on contact. The wind not only blew flames and smoke, but dry leaves which ignited into burning embers. The maelstrom also sent up clouds of sand and dirt.

The Great Fire was now moving irrevocably toward Oconto and the Towsley farm was its next victim. It roared across the twenty acres of withered corn crops, fueled further by the dry, dead stalks. It devoured fences as if they were tiny wooden match sticks. Then it struck the family home and barn at the same moment.

Peshtigo

The barn burned quickly, filled as it was with straw for the horses, cows, and sheep. They all died within seconds, their cries drowned by the howl of the winds.

Just as the fire reached the house, the adults were jarred out of their bed. C.R. ran toward the front of the building but he was mowed down before he got through the hallway. The flames were destroying the walls, the furniture, and the carpets almost instantaneously. Annabelle shrieked as the infrared heat barreled its way into the bedroom, the flames right behind. She heard nothing from her husband, nothing from her children. She was engulfed before she could scream.

The conflagration covered the house for just a few minutes, torching everything in its deadly reach.

C.R. Towsley's remains lay in the hall, his wife and four children all died in their beds. Colleen's frightening dream about the fire's attacking the house and trapping her inside had finally come true.

*   *   *

At the next farm, J.G. Clements was more fortunate. Not only had he been awake and had seen the hurricane of fire coming, he was fully prepared for it.

His wife Felice had convinced him that, with water supplies dwindling, there would be insufficient quantities to fight the fire and save their property. She told him their first priority was to save themselves.

"We can rebuild our home and our barn," she had lectured him. "Our lives we cannot."

So the two had also dug ditches around the house and barn to slow any fires that might storm across the property. But as the weather worsened, Felice told J.G. it was still not enough to protect them.

"Joshua, we must build an underground pit," she told him. "My relatives are doing that up north. They say it will save us no matter how bad the fires are."

The husband and wife had taken their shovels to the side of the barn weeks ago and begun digging a hole under the concrete floor.

It was large enough to hold the two of them. When the excavation was completed, Joshua put several boards over the hole in the ground. The theory was simple: the concrete floor was less likely to burn than the wooden walls or the barn roof.

Of course if the blaze were massive enough, Joshua knew he and his wife might be trapped in the pit, and cooked alive.

He had taken one other precaution by moving one of the water barrels near the opening. If they had enough time to run to the hole, they would soak themselves with water before going underground. It might provide an additional layer of protection.

Now, just after supper on this night of the great fire, J.G. Clements was checking on his animals at the barn. He heard the sound of an approaching train. But there was no train in this rural region. Still, it became louder. He ran outside and beheld the same fire that was obliterating the Towsley property.

"This is it!"

He ran to the house.

"Felice, fire, we must get out!"

She came to the front door and gasped.

"It is so large!" she said. She ran to get blankets.

When she returned, she said, "We should wet these and place them over our heads. A fire that big will burn our skin or it will smother us."

Joshua took the blankets and together they made tracks for the barn. As he removed the planks leading to the pit, she began immersing the blankets, moistening them completely. They waited until the savage fire was close by. Then they threw handfuls of water on each other from head to toe. They kissed, professed their love for one another, and entered the pit.

It took very little time for the fire to march along its destructive path from the Towsley farm. It roared and sputtered and spit flames and sparks, carried by a wind that roared, like a hurricane. The heat was omnipresent and so intense it withered objects before the flames could consume them.

Several miles wide at this point, the inferno was charring a wide swathe of natural vegetation and man-made objects. The Clements property was no exception. The house went first, exploding from the heat and accompanying pressure. Flames darted across the open space, seemingly in search of the barn. There was no hope for the animals inside, who were suffocated before they were burned.

In their subterranean sanctuary, Joshua and Felice huddled together. They heard the ghastly wind, they tasted and breathed the choking smoke, and felt the rising heat. They watched as the huge orange-yellow flames rolled over the hole they had dug.

Above their heads, they detected great thuds, jarring the concrete slab. Joshua whispered to his wife that it was building beams falling to the floor. The heat-level rose rapidly, drying the blankets. Felice feared the fire would linger, and its combined fury would indeed roast them. She could feel the heat on her skin, so intense she thought she felt blisters forming. Joshua had trouble breathing and began coughing. He buried his head into her left armpit, hoping the cough would stop.

The heat suddenly dissipated, the flames moved on, the train roar had passed their hideout. They were still alive and it seemed the worst was over.

Joshua waited as long as he could bear it. He crawled to the edge of the hole and peered out, like some prairie dog in a desert grassland.

Utter destruction.

There was no house.

As he pulled himself out of the pit and looked behind him, he saw to his horror there was no barn. The blaze had leveled the bushes and trees where the fire had just marched through. Stumps smoldered. Smoke was still present. Tears came to Joshua's eyes.

"The fire is gone but it has done its damage," he told her and extended a hand to pull her free of the refuge.

She stood and surveyed the scene.

"It is true," she said. "But I still have you, alive and healthy. We will start again."

"I love you," was all he could say, as tears flowed freely down his smoke-blackened cheeks.

They embraced in the darkness of the after-burn.

"At first light," she told him, "you must go see the Towsleys to be certain all is well with them. For now," she continued, "we need to find a quiet place to get some rest after this ordeal."

Even as Felice Clements spoke, the catastrophic fires pushed on, storming across fields and forest land, hop-scotching the Oconto River in several places. The blazes were bearing down on Peshtigo, about to inflict horrific loss of life to the 'tough little burg' that some had termed the town. Peshtigo was in the path of destruction.

Chapter 8

Another weekend was coming to an end in Peshtigo. The bars and brothels were less busy on this Sunday evening. Business had been brisk for the past two days because several new men had arrived in town, expecting to begin the autumn/winter wood-harvesting cycle.

They came from the Eastern United States and Canada. Others had traveled farther, from Ireland, Germany, and Scandinavia, coming to America to make their fortunes. They had heard or read of the bounteous forests in the upper Midwest, and the big business of taming the forests, bringing riches to shanty boys and even greater riches to the lumber barons. Most of the men arrived by boat because the train line had not been completed. They were often illiterate and those from other nations brought another disability with them, they spoke little or no English. The locals called these newcomers deadheads, people of low intelligence.

During the timber season, there were three men for every woman in Peshtigo and environs. The surplus males spent their idle hours eating, drinking, and waiting their turn at the houses of ill repute.

The rooming houses and hotels were filled, the bars and restaurants had difficulty maintaining supplies, especially in the midst of the drought.

These latest arrivals found something unexpected in this northern climate, at least this year. Rather than being cold and damp, the newcomers experienced warm temperatures, dry conditions, and persistent smoke. They were not accustomed to the hazy air and their lungs soon filled with the smoke. Coughs developed and for some it got worse. Dr. J.F. Kelsey was treating several men for heavy colds and bronchitis.

And there was another danger for newcomer and old-timer alike. Fires that were burning in the wilderness created flaming embers. As winds picked up each afternoon and evening, they hurled the coals into Peshtigo, where they sometimes settled on people's hair or clothing.

As this day came to a close, it was still warm and uncomfortable in the town. The smoke lay heavy across the streets and yards. And, then, just around seven p.m., the wind began to whip up, heaving occasional gusts. The sky was darkening and those in the community who gazed westward saw smoke-filtered rays from the setting sun.

Others seemed ignorant of the weather conditions. It had been like this for so long that tonight seemed no different from any other. These folks walked the streets, laughing or singing or seeking last-minute amusement where they could find it. Many taverns were still open, for those who wanted to extend the weekend as long as possible. Most had had enough. Several men were returning to their temporary lodgings after a day of diversion. Work resumed in the morning.

The perceptive, or the curious, witnessed a brilliant red sunset on this October 8th. And after the sun descended past the horizon, the western sky remained crimson long after dusk, when it normally turned black. This was not right, nor was it normal.

Far off, a gathering roar of wind advanced toward Peshtigo, dull at first, then like an approaching locomotive and finally producing an ear-piercing howl. A veteran of the War Between the States later likened it to a heavy discharge of artillery.

The western edge of the community was victimized first. A furious fire roared into town but, strangely, from above. It seemed to drop from the sky like the remnants of a Fourth of July firebomb. It ignited mini-explosions as the voracious flames attacked desiccated wood chips, feeding the fire's seemingly insatiable appetite. Fire swirls shot back up into the air, enveloping trees and creating flaming columns. Shooting sparks, called fire flakes by some, merely touched off more burning.

The wind became ferocious, blowing nearly forty miles per hour at ground level, gusting at more than sixty miles per hour, hurling objects great distances while pushing the flames faster. The size and speed of the conflagration brought it into town so quickly residents had little or no time to protect themselves. All they could do was try to outrun the force or hide from it.

One of the first Peshtigo families to die didn't get far. A husband and wife carried their 6-year-old daughter to the water well behind their house. The protracted drought had caused the well to run dry. They climbed down a wooden ladder about 20 feet, thinking they would be safe from the fire as it stormed past their house. Soon the flames, the withering heat and thick smoke invaded the property, roaring over the well. The flames did not find the three but the choking smoke did. Within seconds, it cascaded down into the pit, asphyxiating the family in under a minute.

The flames found more fodder every few seconds. Homes, barns, trees, dried grass all went up in smoke. And the casual attitude of the wood men now came back to haunt the town. The piles of wood bits that had been dumped across Peshtigo and wooden particles which blew constantly through town, now provided additional fuel for the inferno.

It also created what some called balloons of fire. They were probably gas bubbles born from the center of the blaze, then set alight by the overwhelming heat. But these balloons were deadly. As they rose toward cooler air, they often exploded, bombarding adjacent areas with sparks. People and animals were struck by them, killed on the spot, like victims of a bombing campaign in a war zone.

*   *   *

Just forty-eight hours earlier, Elias Dix had spent the night on his front porch, watching and waiting, prepared to defend his house from the series of fires that had broken out well beyond his property. His wife Rachel had taken their children into the house where they lay on the floor to avoid the smoke that was drifting through the area.

That experience had unnerved Abram, Martin, Catherine, Iris, and Catelin. The girls had been melancholy for the past two days. And the boys were more subdued than normal. The fires had frightened them all.

Elias and Rachel were concerned. The outbreak so close to them had shown the adults how vulnerable they were. The drier it became, the more susceptible they were to additional fires.

The Dix family had spent a quiet day at home and was preparing for bed. But the preparations were interrupted by the cyclonic roar, an extreme brightness in the western sky, advancing heat and thick, billowing smoke.

A piercing cry went up from one of the children, who happened to be looking through a window. All seven family members hastened to the front door. As they gaped at the approaching firestorm, they had little time to think, or plan.

"Run!" yelled Elias.

He grabbed Catelin and passed her to his wife. He scooped up Iris and Catherine. Abram and Martin were told to run alongside their parents.

The family left the house and raced down the lane to a major road extending east and west. The seven turned east, away from the flames. They joined a stream of residents, fleeing from the west end of Peshtigo who had also chosen to outrun the blaze. Some were alone, with only the clothes they wore, others struggled with bags or suitcases. One woman pulled a child's wagon full of possessions but her speed was constrained because if she went too fast, items would fall out of the wagon or it would topple. One man led a pair of horses. The animals were uncooperative, their eyes suggesting they were frantic. Elias and Rachel were not alone in transporting children. Men and women were holding their offspring. They tended to fall behind the pack, the weight of one or two children in tow slowed their pace.

No one spoke to each other. They were too scared and too concerned about maintaining their escape effort. But there were sounds aplenty: Horses neighing, hooves clattering, tiny wooden wagon wheels rolling along the ground, suitcases dragging across dry ground.

Elias Dix was already tiring. But he had to rally his family.

"We must try to reach the river," he panted to Rachel and the children.

But her stamina was depleting quickly. And the smoky conditions didn't help. She stopped, apparently out of breath. A crowd of people passed them by, heading for safety.

"Keep going!" exhorted Elias.

"I have no breath," Rachel replied. "I must stop for just a minute."

Peshtigo

The boys had run on ahead but, seeing that their parents had stopped, returned to them. The family was now far behind many other evacuees.

"Rachel, please dear, we do not have a minute. We must start again," pleaded Elias.

She began to move again, took a dozen steps and fell under the weight of her baby. Elias came over to help. It was too late.

At that precise moment, the blaze bore down on them. It enfolded the entire Dix family, another group also slowed by children, and the woman with the wagon.

Their shrieks were muffled by the howl of the wind. Then, there was silence. The fire killed a dozen people instantly and left little trace of the victims.

* * *

Maybell Kittner heard the racket from her kitchen. She went out the back door onto the small porch and looked in the direction of the noise. Hordes of people were rushing toward the center of Peshtigo. She hurried around the side of the remodeled wooden home and noticed more people. Then she looked west and saw the cause of the great exodus. A tall wall of fire was burning out of control, chasing people eastward.

She took immediate charge, sprinting into the house and summoning her mother, her sister, and the six children. Fortunately, they were all in the house. As they converged, Maybell announced the news and barked out the orders.

"There is a huge fire blowing this way," she said. "Everyone grab a jacket and go to the front porch. Mother, bring the container with our money. Nan, drag the small trunk with the books and personal papers out onto the porch while I hitch the team to the wagon. Hurry!"

They scattered in every direction. Matriarch Mary got a lined jacket, then retrieved the container in the kitchen cupboard where hundreds of dollars had been stored for emergencies. Nan went to the bedroom she shared with Maybell and took two coats from the closet. Next, she went to the parlor, secured the lock on the trunk, and pulled it across the floor to the front porch. The three boys got their coats and raced to the front porch.

The three girls also grabbed coats, put them on, and made for the front porch to join the rest of the family.

Maybell had scampered off to the combination barn-storage shed, which also housed the family wagon and the two-horse team which pulled it. She deftly brought the animals to the head of the wagon and hitched the horses to the vehicle. She walked up to the horses, patted each on the nose, spoke to them, and led them to the front porch.

Maybell assisted her mother in climbing up onto the wagon seat. Mary would sit in the middle with her daughters on either side of her. Nan made sure all the children got safely into the back of the wagon. Then she and her sister heaved the trunk onto the wagon bed, pushing it into a corner so it would not slide and hit the children, who were crouching behind the buckboard.

"Where is the money?" Maybell asked.

"I have it with me," her mother replied, "close to my heart."

Nan and Maybell jumped aboard the wagon. The elder sister took the reins and urged the horses.

"We will head to the east side of town," Maybell shouted to the rest of the group. "The river may stop the fire so we shall be safe over there."

Maybell was adept at driving the wagon, even though the street was congested with people on foot, horses and wagons, wheelbarrows and handcarts all racing away from the great fire toward the Peshtigo River and the east side of the town. But as she drove on, she encountered so many frightened people in her path that it became more difficult to drive around, or through, them.

"My baby!" a woman shrieked. Maybell drew the horses to a stop.

A young girl, panicked by the pushing crowds, had become separated from her mother. Without thinking, the girl ran toward the middle of the roadway, directly in the path of Maybell's team. She had halted the horses quickly enough.

The child had fallen and now lay on her back, between the two animals, but untouched by them or the wagon wheels. Maybell hopped down from her seat and gathered the child in her arms until her mother approached, snatched the child from Maybell, said nothing, turned, and continued running with the fleeing mob. Maybell returned to the driver's position atop the wagon and got the horses moving again.

Maybell's plan called for her to drive the wagon across the main wooden bridge which connected the two sides of town.

She sensed the spectacular fire was gaining on them. She felt some heat gathering near the back of her neck. As she glanced over her shoulder, Maybell espied the monstrous, churning blaze that was destroying everything in its deadly path.

The sight so chilled her that she goaded her horses to flee even faster. She approached the center of Peshtigo's western shore. As the wagon was turning a corner, another wagon hurtling along the intersecting street sideswiped Maybell. The speed at which both wagons were traveling and the force of the collision knocked Maybell's wagon on its side, hurling all nine of them onto the street. As Mary Kittner fell, the money container she was carrying bounced on the ground. Its lid came loose and the strong wind blew much of the family savings into rising whirlpools that scattered the paper money far and wide. The impact also damaged Mary's right leg and she was unable to stand immediately.

None of the six children was hurt by the fall, nor was Maybell and Nan. But the trunk had been hurled out of the wagon onto the street where it was run over by a huge wagon carrying several people. The lid was thrust open and many of the books were crushed. The personal documents flew away as quickly as the money. But still in the bottom of the trunk was a piece of silk, thus far untouched by other human hands or wagon wheels. Maybell had bought the expensive fabric months before and she planned to make a new Sunday dress from it. She grabbed the silk and stuffed it inside her jacket. She reckoned it might be the only possession she'd still have after the fire roared through town.

Maybell ran quickly to the horses. One had fallen after the wagon was broadsided but it had since returned to its feet and seemed unhurt by the accident. The second horse remained on all-fours and was also unaffected. Noticing that one wagon wheel was shattered and a second was cracked, Maybell knew their ride was over. She decided to unhitch her horses rather than let them suffer in the fire. She also knew, she could not walk them and her entire family to safety.

Sadly, she decided to let them loose. She stroked the face of each one, then smacked their behinds. They took off, heading in the direction of the river. Maybell feared she would never see them again. But now her main concern was her mother, sister, and the children.

Nan had helped Mary to her feet, now displaying a noticeable limp. Mary clutched at the container with what was left of the money.

Maybell concluded it might not be possible to reach the far eastern side of Peshtigo because her mother could hardly walk. But if the family could just get across the bridge onto the other side of the river, it might be safe enough.

The Kittner clan joined the ever-burgeoning throng as it pushed its way to the bridge. Presently, their progress stalled. Soon, they stopped moving altogether. People had to wait for their chance to bolt to freedom.

The crowd murmured. A few shouted.

"Hurry across that bridge so we can get over too!".

"Move quickly or we will all perish!"

"Please keep walking so my children will not die!"

Their pleas were eventually overwhelmed by the sound of the west wind as its force increased. Maybell could not see the approaching fire from where she now stood. Some buildings behind her obscured the view. But she could feel it as the wind shoved the fire's intense heat out ahead of its destructive flames.

"Follow me, everyone," she shouted, tugging on the coat sleeves of her mother and sister. They in turn pulled the children along with them. They left the queue for the bridge.

Maybell Kittner ran down the west bank of the Peshtigo River. She did not stop when she came to the water's edge but plunged into the chilly but calm river. Her family followed, shrieking at the feel of the cold water.

As they looked up and down the length of the waterway, they saw that hundreds of others were also in the river. Many were fording the stream and pushing to the opposite shore. Others had decided to stay put, figuring the moisture might protect them if the fire should reach the river.

"Swim across," Maybell told Nan, "and take Mother with you."

Nan began her watery journey. The children were standing waist-deep in the water, shivering, shedding a few tears, dazed by what was transpiring.

"Asa, Richard, I know you can swim," their mother said. "Can you take one of the younger children with you?"

They said they could so Maybell assigned Asa to take his sister Clair across the water. She gave Richard custody of cousin John. Maybell grabbed Sara and began swimming across.

A quarter-hour later, they had all reached the eastern side without difficulty. They were soaked and shivering. Maybell stopped them as they stood on the riverbank.

"I think we should stay here," she said. "If the fire gets larger and hotter, we may need to get into the water. I know we are all wet and cold but I think the heat of the fire will actually dry our clothes. We will be safer here by the water."

And there they remained, waiting and watching for the most destructive fire they had ever witnessed to bear down on them.

* * *

On the northwest edge of town, a stream meandered westward, a branch of the Peshtigo River. The water level was lower than it would have been in a year with normal rainfall. But as the tragedy befell the town, the river proved a life-saver.

As the wall of fire spread and targeted Peshtigo, the stream became a refuge for those living nearby. As residents saw the cataclysmic fire coming, they just had time to run for the stream.

But the families had no time to grab valuables or get the horses and wagons ready for their escape. Men and women assembled their children and sprinted away from the approaching holocaust.

Some fifty adults and children were streaking toward the stream, hoping the water would stop the fire or at least protect them from the flames and the intense heat. A few were running so fast, they fell but were able to pick themselves up and continue their frenzied race for the safety of the stream.

The smoke blew out ahead of the fire, a presage of the destructive force that lay just behind it. It was a choking haze that made people cough and gag, so thick that some people could not see where they were or where they were going. A few women were overcome by the pall of smoke but were carried or dragged to the water's edge.

The sound of the wind was almost drowned by other very distinct sounds: Screams and wails from those frightened by the approaching blaze and who were anxious to reach the safety of the water, splashing sounds from those who reached the stream, ran in, and waded toward the center of the creek. And then they became aware of yet another sound.

Groans and whines came from a herd of cows as they stampeded toward the water, their instinct telling them the river might save them from harm. Fourteen terrified cows were intent on self-preservation, as were the humans. The cows ran faster in their fear. They knew the water was not far off. They had to get there before the fire touched them.

Some of the women and children were no match for the careening cattle.

"No, no!" cried out two women in unison, carrying children toward the water.

As the animals swept past them, the women and children were knocked down by the cattle. The herd trampled the four humans and plunged into the water. The women and children lay motionless in their wake.

A tornado-like sound heralded its arrival near the water. The heavy cloud of smoke came first. As it approached, the people ducked under the water. Some had to come up for air while the haze still enveloped them so they submerged themselves a second time. The smoke had barely cleared when the shooting flames stormed toward the water.

The intensity of the heat made the victims dive under the water once again. When their lungs ached and they had to surface, the massive fire was still close by. Indeed, it was walking across the water. One man bellowed as he was engulfed in flames so fierce they melted his skin in a matter of seconds. The bodies of two young children bobbed on top of the water. They had tried to stay underwater but had drowned rather than surface in the midst of the flames.

A man and his wife who had managed to avoid the smoke and the flames by bobbing in and out of the stream had to fend off another attack. The body of a cow, asphyxiated by the smoke, floated down the stream. The woman became trapped under the animal and her husband used all his strength to dislodge her. As she began to cry uncontrollably, her husband shook her.

"Stop it! Control yourself!" he shouted. "We need to go under again so the heat will not burn us."

When they resurfaced, they beheld another disgusting sight. The blackened bodies of men, women, children, and cattle were floating all around them. The heat remained overwhelming so the couple once again sought safety on the stream bottom for as long as their lungs would allow.

"Is anyone here?" the man called, when they had surfaced once more.

At first, he heard no voices, only the sound of the flames shooting high into the air in every direction. Gradually, though, others responded. People called out and came together. Those who had survived tried to comfort one another as the fire moved past them. Four men, three women, and two children, all were strangers. In fact, none of the nine was related to anyone else in the small survivor group.

With the searing heat past them, the survivors began to realize how cold and damp they were in the water. But no one dared move until they were certain the fire was gone. The men took the initiative, introducing themselves and asking the women and children their names. The males said they would stay in the water just a bit longer, then recommended the remainder of the group leave the water and rest on the bank. The risk of fire seemed to have diminished, the men said. But the women and children were frightened to leave the safety of their moist retreat, especially if other fires blew in. They wanted to remain there for the night. In the morning, they could begin the grim task of searching for loved ones and perhaps return to their homes to see if anything survived.

But as they huddled in the creek, they detected a brightening behind them. They turned, aghast to realize that large sections of burning debris were floating toward them. In fact, the fiery planks extended the entire width of the waterway. An upstream building along the bank had fallen into the water and flaming pieces of it were sailing directly at the small group of survivors.

They began to scramble to the shore. Some slipped and lost their footing. Others tried to run and swim at the same time. It was no use. The blazing debris was moving too fast. It either knocked them down into the water and kept them submerged until they could no longer breathe or the heat and flames attacked them. A man holding one of the children was upended by a pair of flaming logs. He and the child fell on top of the logs and were burned to death. A woman was knocked unconscious by one plank. She fell into the water and drowned.

The debris continued burning as it floated past the site where the nine had gathered in refuge.

Silence.

There were no voices calling out for the others. All nine had perished.

*   *   *

Near the center of Peshtigo, the sound of church bells competed with the roar of the wind.

A parishioner of the Congregational Church ran inside the building and began sounding the bell, as an alarm that fire was approaching rapidly from the west. Another man rang a second bell, this one at the roofless Catholic church. The bell tower had been completed and the bell set in place just prior to the final construction on the rest of the edifice. The sentinels at both churches vowed to continue until the fires forced them to leave. But they took comfort in the fact that their efforts may have been useful to their fellow citizens.

Several people, on hearing the sound at this odd hour, looked out of doors and windows and became aware of the approaching cataclysm. Many had time to gather belongings before making a mad dash toward the Peshtigo River or across the town bridge.

T.A. Hay heard the bells while reading in his town center apartment, on the floor above his jewelry shop. He went to his open living room window and noticed the bright light in the western sky, and the strengthening wind which was now increasing in volume. On the street below he watched as groups of people rushed down his street in the direction of the bridge, just two blocks from his business. With the realization that danger was on his doorstep, T.A. Hay made his move.

He was single and had no family. He needed only to save himself. And he needed to save as much of his business as he could. The jeweler grabbed a coat from a rack in his hall, then ran down the stairway from his living quarters to his livelihood. In the dark, he fumbled from case to case, grabbing as many valuable items as he could, stuffing them into a cloth sack he kept in his kitchen for groceries. Then he headed for the back of the shop. His targets were the expensive gold and diamond rings and a select grouping of pearl necklaces which he had ordered from Chicago and which had arrived just three weeks ago. As he worked, the sound outside grew louder. Not many voices but there was the drone of people running, of horses galloping past, of wagon loads of people and possessions making their escape. The overwhelming sound was similar to a hurricane, as the wind-driven fires raced toward the center of the community.

A great torrid gust blew down Oconto Street in the center of Peshtigo. It was so strong it knocked adults off their feet. It threw young children against the walls of buildings.

Crash!

It shattered one of the two plate glass windows of the Hay jewelry shop. T.A. Hay was so frightened by it, he dropped to the floor, sheltering the bag of goods beneath him and burying his face in the floor while his arms covered his head and ears. The haze and heat were now ushered in through the open space. The businessman knew there was no more time to snatch his precious possessions. He picked himself up, ran to the locked door of his shop, forced it open, and joined the growing throng running eastbound to the bridge and to the river.

He had gone no more than a block when he realized how many people were jammed up at the bridge. They had to wait until those on the structure walked across to the east side of town. He considered it suicidal to wait so he followed the course others were taking and ran to the river's edge, seeking shelter in the cool, moist waters of the Peshtigo. Before wading into the water, T.A. loosened his belt and forced the top of his sack under the belt. He hoped that when he re-tightened the belt, it would prevent the sack from sinking. He would also hold it but he wanted a backup plan in case his hands were needed for other lifesaving pursuits.

The jeweler walked slowly and carefully into the river, edging toward deeper water. He felt cooler, more comfortable here. When he reached shoulder level, he stopped. With one hand on his treasure bag, T.A. bent his knees and went below the surface. The heat remained above the water line. The acrid smoke was no longer choking his lungs. If he could stay in this place, moving up and down in the water, he might be able to protect himself from the flames, the smoke, and the hell of heat. When he came back up for air, his moistened skin and clothing protected him. But that was short-lived. He could see the massive conglomeration of flames charging toward the river. The smoke was thicker now, the heat more pronounced. T.A. realized his face was not just dry but it was beginning to burn from the fire. Quickly, he re-immersed himself to escape the mounting danger.

Up again. He noticed what seemed like hundreds of people rushing to the river, hurling themselves into the water. Down again.

When he surfaced, he saw he was no longer alone; in fact, he was surrounded. People were pouring into the Peshtigo and competing for places in the comforting water. A few men came near him and T.A. Hay became defensive.

"That is close enough," he said. "Keep your distance so we all have room to wet ourselves under the water."

The men abided by his request and gave him several feet of clearance. But as the throngs threw themselves into the river, none of the men knew how long they could maintain the distance.

T.A. went under for another dunking, then came back up. He looked toward the wooden bridge, which was lit by the torches and candles of others seeking salvation on the far side of the river. Slowly the crowds moved across the span. The queue to cross stretched well back along Oconto Street and the fire blew ever closer. Those at the end of the line gave up and took their chances in the river, rather than walking above it. When T.A. looked to the eastern side of the waterway, he noticed those who had made it across dispersed in several directions. They must have sensed the fire was too big, too powerful to be stopped by the river so they continued their efforts to outrun it.

T.A. Hay went under yet again. He tried to stay down longer because the heat had become so intolerable that it dried his face as soon as he surfaced. Up again.

He decided to remove his coat, even though it was damp and heavy, and drape it over his head. This would protect him from the withering heat. He also discovered that by dipping the coat in the water and placing it on his head, it saved him from the near-constant need of going under water for as long as his lungs would hold out. He was amazed how rapidly the coat dried out from the fire and he was scared. The entire sky was illuminated by a wave of fire that extended for blocks. Flames soared at least a hundred feet into the October sky. The inferno moved quickly, devouring homes, businesses, barns, fences, wooden sidewalks. The more it consumed, the more potent it became. Despite the fire's heat, T.A. was shivering. It could not have been the river water because the heat had warmed it. He was shivering because the entire world was ablaze and he was afraid it was about to consume him and others in the river.

The fire moved brazenly, albeit slowly through the town. More people crammed into the water, closing in on T.A. Hay, and trying to protect themselves from immolation. They screamed, cried, whimpered, moaned. And they doused themselves continually, hoping and praying this nightmare would end soon.

*   *   *

David and Priscilla Maxon were sick in bed at their home not far from the Peshtigo River. It was some type of fever. Priscilla came down with it first and had been laid up for several days. David had contracted it from her a few days ago although he knew he was less ill than his wife. He just needed to rest. He thought he might take a sick day from his job at The Peshtigo Company tomorrow if he didn't improve overnight.

Priscilla was sleeping soundly, perspiring from the medicine she'd been given by the doctor. But signs were good because her fever seemed lower, her skin less hot to the touch. Perhaps, David thought, she was nearly over it. He was not asleep. Just resting in the approaching darkness on this Sunday evening.

The noise began slowly but built quickly. David opened his eyes, trying to place the origin of the sound. Over time, it became louder. Then, the church bell began to chime. It forced him to get up and move unsteadily toward the front door. As he opened it, his five children joined him in peeking out.

They were greeted by a pall of heavy smoke and a stream of people heading through town.

"Adam, go out and ask someone about this," he told his eldest son.

The boy did not hesitate but ran across the front lawn to the street. He stopped a man who was carrying a large satchel over his shoulder. The two conversed for several seconds, looked to the West, then the man walked on quickly and Adam raced back to the house. Even before he reached the porch, David Maxon could see flames pushing high into the western sky and he could feel the wind increasing its fury as it pushed the fire in the direction of his house.

"Fire, father," the boy announced. "The man says a great fire is burning the western part of town and is moving this way. He says we should leave."

"Quickly, children," David ordered. "Get a coat and hat and come back into this room, while I wake your mother. We will have to move her even though she is ill."

Adam, his brothers Caleb and Zebadee went to their room while Mary and Tess ran to the bedroom they shared. David went to his own room, put on a jacket while grabbing one for his wife. He went to the bed to nudge her. Pulling her to a sitting position, David put the coat over Priscilla's shoulders.

"Priscilla, there is a huge fire blowing this way from the west," he told his still-groggy wife. "We must get out of the house."

David picked her up in his arms and carried Priscilla to the front room. The children were already assembled there. David no longer felt sick. He knew he must take charge of his family's escape before the inferno reached them.

Peshtigo

"Follow me to the river," he said. "Adam, you carry Zeb. Caleb, you follow your brothers and, Mary, take Tess' hand and stay close to me."

There was no time to gather any of their belongings. David Maxon hauled his sickly wife and led his children toward the shore of the Peshtigo River. He went around the side of the house, through a back garden, then through some neighbors' properties until they came to the riverside.

"Everyone in the water," he commanded, "and wade out until the water is quite high. Do as those other folks are doing."

Scores of people were already in the river, dousing themselves, covering their heads with moistened towels, blankets, and coats. All five Maxon children were hesitant about wading toward the river's midpoint.

"Come on," he shouted over the din of the rising fire-wind.

They walked out about fifteen feet into water David considered deep enough. He put Zebadee on Adam's shoulders. Then he put his wife into the water and told her to lean against their oldest son. He noticed Priscilla was now shivering in the cool water, even with her fever. She was very wobbly but Adam held her firmly.

"Your mother cannot stand here until the fire threat passes," he told his offspring. "I will run back to the house to bring something for her."

"Oh, Daddy, no," cried Mary, "you may not make it back if the fire reaches our house."

But David was already pushing his way toward the shore, oblivious to his daughter's supplication.

He retraced his steps through the yards he had crossed to reach the river. At length, he arrived at his own house, pushed the closed front door open, and ran into the dark house. Without hesitation, he went to the boys' room and grabbed the small bed used by baby Zebadee. There were two blankets on the bed and he left them there. Turning the bed on its side, he forced it through the bedroom door and along the hall to the front room. He opened the door again and carried the bed through the door onto the front porch. As he edged his way down the porch steps, he kicked an object. It was a wooden pail, kept there to moisten the outside walls of the house.

It was too late for that. He felt the fire, then he looked up and saw its churlish flames blowing toward his neighborhood. Thick smoke completed the misery. David could barely breathe and he could hardly see the street. But he could hear the sound of more people trying to escape the conflagration.

David decided to slide the pail's rope handle over one shoulder as he hoisted the small bed and held it close to his side. He began edging his way slowly toward the river once more.

It took twice as long to get there with his baggage but he managed to find his family among the gathering throng of Peshtigans seeking safety in the water.

"Father, over here!" shouted Mary when she saw him at the river bank.

He slogged back into the water but traveled only about half the distance to his wife and children. He set the bed in a place where the water rose just to the top of the mattress. David grabbed the blankets before the water carried them away. He waded out to get his wife, picked her up again, and carried her back to the small bed. The children followed him.

Setting her down, he doused the blankets in river water and covered her. The children surrounded their mother's sick bed.

"We will take turns filling this bucket and pouring on Mother's blankets to keep her from getting burned," David instructed them. "And I want you children to take your coats off, wet them, and put them over your heads so you will not be burned either."

As their garments were already wet, the children had to struggle to remove the coats. Adam took the lead, placing his coat over his head. The others followed. At first they laughed at the sight they made. But the laughter faded quickly.

David dropped down into the river, covering his face with water. He surfaced, removed his own coat, and threw it over his head. He then dipped the pail into the water and began moistening the blankets covering Priscilla. He made sure her face and head were under the covers so they would not be burned or scarred once the fire got closer.

As its violent intensity grew, David Maxon noticed his coat was drying rapidly. The smoke and heat sucked the dampness out of it. He dropped to his knees, put the coat back into the river, and soaked himself and the garment. He noticed his children's coats were also dry.

"Children, as soon as your coats dry, wet them again and again," he yelled over the rising tornadic wind.

He poured more water over the bed again and looked toward the water's edge. A column of fire perhaps fifty feet high and stretching all along the bank was gnawing its way toward the river, and his family. Choking, billowing smoke jumped even higher. The inferno was pushed mercilessly forward by a wind so strong it knocked two of the younger children over into the water. David grabbed Caleb when he went under. Adam put baby Zeb on the bed momentarily and reached for Mary who had fallen on her back.

"Hold onto the bed," David ordered, "and keep your coats wet."

As all the Maxons held onto the bed, the fire came closer. It resembled a great and wide waterfall of flame, consuming buildings, wagons, trees, and now the grass near the water's edge, turning everything black, reducing it to ash. The blaze approached the river. David prayed the Peshtigo might slow its progress or put it out so his family would be saved.

* * *

By now thousands of men, women, children, and animals were running for their lives. Given the intensity of the fire, they had concluded there was only one way to run, eastward, away from the rolling, rumbling firestorm. The evacuees also knew there was no place to hide, so they opted for the same escape hatch, across the river to the eastern side of Peshtigo, or into the river itself.

Through it all, there was a cacophony of sounds. The howling of the fire-feeding wind, the explosions as the inferno's heat caused objects to explode, the clatter of shoes and boots and horse's hooves clomping the ground as people retreated from the fire's wrath, and the sloshing sounds as residents ran frantically into the river and pushed as far away from the fire as possible.

Strangely, there were few sounds from the people themselves. They were in such shock they said almost nothing. Their minds raced as they plotted their escape route, their tongues were tied from fright.

The river bridge issued its own sounds. The thumping of its wooden planks from the constant crossing of man and beast. The squeaking of the bridge, as the weight of vast crowds put pressure on its structural soundness. And the voice of one Peshtigo fireman, urging crossers to remain calm and keep moving so others could follow behind them.

Many carried lanterns to light their way. They were surrounded by a stark blackness on both sides, although they knew the river was just below and they could hear the sounds of those who had taken refuge in the cool dark water. One man, waiting for the line to move across the span leaned over the side railing, holding his lantern before him. The river below seemed to have disappeared. All he could see was crowds of people, shoulder-to-shoulder, wetting themselves and their clothes and trying to save themselves from asphyxiation or incineration. Adults and children, horses and dogs, furniture and wagons had all entered the watery respite.

As the Great Peshtigo Fire forged a deadly trail through the town, the citizens became even more fearful. They pushed and shoved, trying to move people faster across the sole bridge. The lucky ones continued running once they reached the eastern shore.

Among that crowd was J.F. Kelsey, Peshtigo's physician. As soon as it became clear that a catastrophe was developing, Dr. Kelsey decided the time had come to stop saving others and worry about saving himself. Donning a hat and coat and taking a special envelope containing hundreds of dollars in cash from his desk drawer, the doctor sprinted to the bridge, elbowed his way through the dazed and confused crowd, and continued his voyage through the town, following the main road north to the town of Marinette. J.F. offered no help, nor any words of comfort to anyone. His mission was to escape. When he chanced upon a woman and child nearly trampled by the crush of the crowd, he ignored them and continued his hasty retreat. The woman and girl, he decided, must fend for themselves or suffer the consequences.

Doctor Kelsey had left his traveling medical bag behind. His would run or walk the six or so miles to Marinette, where he thought he could board one of the ships in the port, and escape this cataclysm as the boat cast off and sailed out into the Green Bay and then to Lake Michigan.

Peshtigo

J.F. had not thought what he would do after that. He might return to Peshtigo someday. But for now, he knew he needed to get away, had to run for his freedom. He had been busy treating a growing horde of patients. He must now leave them and the town behind. He had money. He could go to Green Bay, Milwaukee, Chicago, or back east. He might never return to Peshtigo.

*   *   *

For John Cox, the butcher's assistant, an enjoyable weekend had come to a precipitous and perilous end. He and two friends had spent Friday night drinking beer, dining on beef, and dwelling on the stuff of their lives. The three had talked and laughed until the early hours of Saturday. Rising late, John went off to the wooded area where he practiced his bow and arrow until late afternoon. Back in his own place by sundown, John Cox made himself a small dinner of beans, pork, bread, and beer. He'd gone to bed early, to make up for the late night before.

Rested, he awoke early on Sunday, had some coffee and bread and attended church services. After church, he stopped by the bakery to purchase some fresh rolls. He managed to get the last three. The baker told him supplies of flour were harder to come by and water was becoming scarce. The baker said he might have to close down for a week or so if the weather did not improve quickly.

Back in his apartment, John Cox had a roll and cheese for lunch. As he ate, he read over the latest edition of the local newspaper. The updates on the weather did nothing to cheer him. By mid-afternoon, John Cox decided the news of the day had depressed him enough. So he trudged back to his forested area, pulled his bow string and hurled arrows into a target and some tree trunks. He had challenged himself and realized this practice had tired him more than most. Breathing seemed harder and he noticed the smoky smell in the air seemed thicker, more pronounced. But it had been like this on and off for so long, John ignored the climate for the most part.

As the blazing sun sank and the day's light faded, a perspiring John Cox gathered up his arrows and began the trek home. His Peshtigo neighborhood seemed eerily quiet when he returned. His dinner of leftover pork and beans, along with another of the fresh bakery rolls, was barely finished when he detected a dull sound. But it was getting louder quickly. He rose from his dining table and walked to the front door.

"Great God!" he muttered.

Hordes of people were rushing toward his home. They ran, sat in wagons, or rode on horseback. Some carried lanterns to light their way. Others charged ahead in the fast-approaching darkness.

"What is it?" he yelled to passers-by.

"Fire!" a woman said, as she panted past his door. "It is destroying everything in its path. Run!"

He took the stranger's advice. He locked his door, wondering whether that would be necessary, especially if the fire were huge and might burn down his home anyway. Then, John Cox joined the mushrooming throng. He wasn't certain where he was going.

A man spoke up. "You must run eastward to escape. I am going to the river, either across the bridge or I will swim across the water. I hope the river will stop the fire but it is a monster."

John's progress, as well as the hundreds he had just joined, was now reduced from a run, to a jog, then a walk, finally a stall. As the crowd inched forward, many lost their temper and began shouting to those farther ahead.

"Hurry up there! Move along. We all need to cross the river."

John decided to break free of the slow-moving queue. He thought he might avoid the group which appeared aimed for the Peshtigo River bridge and get to the water's edge and the safety the river might provide. But many others had come to a similar conclusion so now the crowd ducking between buildings was as thick as it was on the town's streets.

From behind him, John Cox heard the crescendo of plaintive cries.

"Hurry, please hurry. Push!"

But the crowds ahead of him remained motionless. They had no place to go. All had to wait until those on the bridge had passed across it and those breaking for the river bank actually got into the water safely.

Fear gripped the rear flanks as people heard, saw, and smelled the raging fire moving dangerously closer to them. A massive shove began from the back and pushed several folks farther forward. Some lost their balance and fell, which made progress toward the bridge even slower. People from the back continued pushing and more people went down, especially women and children who could not stand up to the heavy onslaught from behind.

John Cox was pushed by the force of the crowd but he did not totter forward. He moved quickly to his right to avoid the next wave of pushing. Now he was free of the crush of the crowd. As he attempted to accelerate his pace toward the river, a woman was knocked sideways and fell directly into his path. He stopped short, then bent down to help her regain her footing.

In the dark, he saw her face. And he noticed her auburn hair. Then a spark of recognition flashed through the tears in her eyes.

"I know you," he said. "We passed each other outside the butcher shop on Friday evening."

"Yes, I thought it was you," she whimpered. "Please help me."

Without another word, he pulled her to her feet, a task made more difficult as scores of people rushed past them. When she was standing, he put an arm around her shoulder.

"Come with me so we can escape all this. My name is John Cox. I will help you."

"Thank you so much, Mister Cox," she said through tears of terror.

"My name is Kate Guillfoyle. I thought it was you. I hoped it was you. I am so glad it is you."

John guided her toward the Peshtigo River. They said nothing. He had decided the only salvation lay in getting to the water and getting into it. Kate's fears remained, even under his protective strength. She shivered in the growing heat, from fear.

Finally, John revealed his plan.

"We have to get into the water if we can find a place. It is our only chance."

Kate Guillfoyle did not utter a word. She merely gazed up into his face and nodded. Then her lips trembled for a few seconds.

"Thank you," she said, "I will never forget you."

John Cox only smiled. Then he tightened his grip around her shoulder and hurried her along to the river's edge. The water gave off a reddish-orange reflection. John turned behind him to see the massive fire roaring and rising and running straight for the river.

George Bauer

*   *   *

At 7 p.m., Father Peter Pernin left his small home to visit a neighbor. Aldina Dress was a sixty-five-year-old widow. The older woman and younger man walked around her back yard, engaging in conversation. A sudden gust of wind blew in from the west, bothering both of them. But they tried to ignore it, as this type of meteorological phenomenon had become so ordinary in the past several weeks.

But some twenty minutes later, a burst of wind caught their attention. Father Pernin looked up and noticed an old oak tree had caught fire. Sparks and burning cinders had blown into Aldina's property and set the tree alight. The priest sprinted to the tree, grabbed a fallen limb, and began beating at the flames and the burning leaves. He managed to shake them loose and they drifted to the ground. By this time, Aldina had joined him and the pair began stomping at the smoldering vegetation. They soon extinguished the flames and the threat of more serious fire.

As unexpectedly as it had arrived, the wind now diminished, then disappeared. Father Pernin walked Mrs. Dress back to her house, bid her good night, and returned to his own quarters. But a feeling of disquiet nagged at him and he decided after a few minutes to go outside once more. Looking westward, the priest now saw a dense cloud of smoke and a massive red reflection in the evening sky. And he heard a distant roaring sound.

He uttered a prayer for protection, after concluding that a major blaze was not far off. He realized there was not time to gather many possessions. He got what he could, then raced to his storage tunnel, uncovered it, and deposited the valuables–books, clothing, church ornaments. He shoveled the sand and dirt over the now-closed vault.

His horse was tied to a tree near the house. Father Pernin untied the animal and smacked its behind. The horse would have a better chance of survival, he thought, if it could run away on its own, not held back by the priest.

The fireball grew even brighter and the roar became even more pronounced. He thought of a lengthy train rumbling toward a station, deafening as it squealed to a stop.

Another neighbor, Edna Tyler, left her home and approached him. She and her husband had been entertaining guests, serving an early evening high tea. The guests had departed only minutes before.

"Father," is there any danger?"

"I do not know," he replied, "but I have unpleasant premonitions and feel that I should prepare for trouble."

"But if a fire breaks out," she pressed him, "what are we to do?"

"Seek the river at once," was his response.

Edna Tyler returned to her house. She and her husband assembled their four children rapidly and rushed in the direction of the river.

Peter Pernin then followed his own advice. But before departing he called his dog, who was lying near his rectory.

"Run, Jeremiah, run," he commanded and the dog took off.

Father Pernin raced into the unfinished church and grabbed the tabernacle, where the Blessed Sacrament is kept. He stumbled toward his wagon, set the tabernacle down into the wagon bed. Now he held the most important object for any Catholic priest..the repository for the body of Jesus Christ. He darted to the front of his wagon and began pulling it toward the Peshtigo River. After he left, he did not know it but his dog Jeremiah returned from a hiding place and resumed his position near the rectory.

As he lurched forward, Peter Pernin approached a tavern. He had never approved of the place because he knew it drew men like a magnet at all times of the day or night, even on Sundays when he was saying Mass. When he passed by, he heard voices inside, hoots and howls coming from patrons seemingly oblivious to the danger on their doorstep. Father Pernin uttered a silent prayer for the men inside as he trudged on. He had not gone a block when a frightening explosion jolted him. The priest stopped, turned halfway around, and noticed that the bar he'd just passed had caught fire and blown apart. There seemed nothing left of the structure. The priest concluded that no one inside could have survived.

Now the inferno was literally breathing down his neck, so Father Pernin strained and pulled his cart faster, or as fast as he could, given the crowds in the street trying to escape. The river lay just a few streets away. But the approaching firestorm brought with it furnace-like heat and inhumane winds. It sounded like a hurricane, he thought. And he discovered how difficult it was to breathe, the air now filled with sand, wood chips, ashes, cinders, and sparks.

The wind roared as the fire raced, the flames crackled as they destroyed homes and other buildings, those fleeing the fire coughed and wheezed as they endured the choking smoke. It was getting ever closer. The priest pulled with renewed vigor until he reached the waterfront.

Peter Pernin knew he had to cross the Peshtigo River to safety. But as he ambled toward the town bridge, he was horrified to see that the fire was moving directly toward the structure. The bridge would soon catch fire along with the rest of the western part of the town. Nevertheless, scores of people continued to cross the span, hoping to beat the charging blaze.

Father Pernin decided to make for the river itself, as had hundreds of residents before him. As he dragged his cargo toward the water, he looked to his right. The Peshtigo Company sawmill, one of the landmarks of the community, was now ablaze. The Great Peshtigo Fire was now like some monstrous flaming vise, tightening its grip around the fleeing residents.

At the edge of the water, Peter Pernin found a long line of frightened people, staring blankly at the fire-lightened sky. Several feet away, he saw a woman, a stranger to him, out of breath, dragging a young child to the river for safety. With the other, she held what appeared to be an infant wrapped in a blanket. At the thought of safety, she sighed and prepared to take her children into the water. She unwrapped the blanket.

"No!!" she shrieked. The baby was not there. Father Pernin could only conclude that the child has slipped out of its mother's arms as she raced for the security of the river. The woman entered the water, crying inconsolably. The priest noticed that those around her attempted to console the ailing mother. He then came upon a man who seemed paralyzed with fear, unable to move. The priest pushed him into the river, then entered the warming water himself, dragging the wagon with the sacred tabernacle behind him. Now in the river, the dazed man yelled at the priest.

"I am wet" he cried.

Then he thought better of his condition, realizing Father Pernin had come to his aid.

"But better surrounded by the water than consumed by the fire."

Peter Pernin waded in deeper, up to his neck. But the water would not protect him. Unbelievably, the flames had reached the river, even entered it. Fueled by wagons, wooden furniture, and heat-dried clothing, the fire raced along the waterway crammed with people.

There were screams and moans from those in the fire's path.

Before some could drop into the water to fend off the flames, the fire attacked them. It moved quickly, engulfing men, women, and children, entire families, in a matter of seconds. As the fire pushed on, it left a stream of human and animal bodies bobbing in the turgid water of the river. Heavier metal objects sank to the river bottom. But some charred wood floated downstream.

Father Pernin had managed to get himself toward the middle of the river. He had to keep submerging himself as huge tongues of flame continued licking the western river's edge, consuming everything. When he surfaced for air, Peter Pernin became truly frightened. He saw fire in every direction, flames racing higher and higher into the night sky. And, now, the bridge was ablaze. The inferno mowed down the people trying to cross the span. Then it covered them in crimson flames and smoke. The dry wood of the bridge and its upper supports burned rapidly.

A huge wooden pylon from the structure had toppled and was drifting toward Peter Pernin's group of survivors. The priest knew his only chance to survive was not just to slip under the water but to dive down to the bottom until the flaming chunk of bridge passed by. He stayed below as long as his lungs would hold out. But when he surfaced, there were new and additional dangers. People and animals fleeing the burning bridge pushed him over several times in their desperate escape attempts. More debris passed by. A man next to him had gone underwater to re-moisten himself. But as he resurfaced, a burning log hit him in the head and dragged him back under the water. Father Pernin went to pull the man up but he was no longer there. Pernin dived down to locate the man but he was gone. The priest assumed the man had been dragged away by the log. He never saw the man again.

Behind him, a woman screamed. Two red-hot metals hoops, probably used to hold wooden barrels together had floated into her. She went under the water line and did not return. In the air, Father Pernin detected the foul odor of burned flesh. He murmured yet another prayer, then dived a second time. He found her limp body on the floor of the river and hauled her up but when he broke water and called to her, there was no response.

She was dead so he let go of her and she slid back down into the black water.

*   *   *

When the conflagration reached the Peshtigo bridge, it attacked the structure quickly and mercilessly. Hundred-foot-high flames were pushed by the wind directly at the wooden span. Like some gaping maw, the fire seemed to consume the bridge in a fiery gulp, obliterating everyone and everything. Then hundreds of people stuck on the bridge had no recourse. It happened so fast, they were unable even to hurl themselves over the side and into the river. The force of the inferno blasted wooden beams and planks into splinters. The explosion sent a rain of fire back down into the river and along its edges. Not only did those on the bridge die but several people nearby were also incinerated.

So now there was no escape route by foot from west to east. Evacuees had to ford the river to safety. And the east side of Peshtigo was no longer a safe haven. By ten p.m., the relentless fire had skipped across the river and darted across the bridge. It began destroying that part of the community.

The eastside residents who had watched in horror as their over-the-river neighbors tried to escape the onslaught were now victims themselves. They had more warning, more time to prepare an escape. And some East-siders felt they were safe, assuming the river would stop the fire before it reached them. But the fire catapulted the river so fast, many were forced to run for their lives.

The flames raced in three directions as the forceful wind continued to spread the blast furnace from the west. But the inferno now raced to the east, north, and northeast. Its speed confounded and intimidated everyone as it raced to new neighborhoods. New victims concluded they had to get away from buildings, trees, and brush. In one northern precinct, more than sixty people converged in an open corn field. As the unholy roar bore down on them, they decided to huddle together amid some large boulders at the edge of the field.

"We must crouch down behind these rocks on the side that is away from the fire and we must cover ourselves with our coats or other clothing," one man said.

The crowd had little time to prepare. The howling blaze danced swiftly along the tops of several trees that skirted the farm field. Then, as some destroyed trees toppled, the flames ignited the dry grasses and corn stalks on the ground. It moved straight toward the boulders, its cyclonic roar announcing its deadly arrival.

Flames shot fifty feet into the sky. On the ground, corn stalks propelled hot sparks, like some children's holiday sparklers. They in turn ignited more corn. The fire was now in a low-level feeding frenzy.

Two-thirds of the field now lay blackened and barren. There was no hint in the ashes that corn or grass had ever grown there. And at the edge of the field, the rocks were reduced to rubble and cinders. And sixty-eight people lay dead, burned beyond recognition. The fire had devoured the field in four minutes.

Not far away, other residents took immediate refuge in Trout Creek. The longstanding drought had lowered the water level but the creek had not run dry. Some thirty people raced into what water was left. It was just enough to cover all those seeking shelter. When the fire arrived, they held their breath and went under, hoping and praying it would be enough. One of them was John Mulligan, a railway crew boss and a former prize-fighter. He carried his wife Monica on his back to Trout Creek, to what he hoped was safety. She wore only a silky nightgown. Even submerged, the heat of the fire made the nightgown burn. It burned off her body but the water which surrounded her prevented serious injuries. John removed his jacket and gave it to his naked wife, who was burned and frightened but still alive.

When the danger had passed them by, all thirty people who had sprinted for the water emerged into the blackness of the night. Every one of them had survived in the safety of Trout Creek.

But Isaiah Hill and his family were less fortunate. He managed about 50 acres of farmland near Trout Creek, while his wife Margaret managed the couple's eight children. The Hill farm had been productive in years past, when nearly all the acreage bulged with corn or wheat, and alfalfa in some years. But the 1871 crop had been a disaster, mirroring the disappointment of most farms in Northern Wisconsin.

Isaiah had become so frustrated by the weather that he had given up on the current corn crop in September. He no longer even went out to scan his fields and their yields. The corn was dry, dying, and withering. It would mean that the Hills would have to dip into their meager savings to make it through the winter. Margaret would have to stretch the food allotments. And the entire family would have to conserve water. They could still rely on the creek but its level was falling. Isaiah was not certain it would last many months longer.

A depression settled over the family. The five boys and three girls had become sullen. They complained constantly that they were hungry because they were in fact not getting enough to eat.

Margaret was forlorn. She spent the days washing and mending clothes and trying to make meals for ten people with very little in the larder. She ordered the girls to clean the house after school and study time. They had other chores on weekends. The boys helped their father mending fences, repairing and maintaining tools, and hauling water from Trout Creek to the farmhouse.

On this evening, the Hill family consumed its dinner in virtual silence. Most of them were not interested in more talk about the drought, the heat, the failed crop, and the depleting food supply.

When dinner was done and the kitchen was cleaned, Isaiah said everyone should sit together in the parlor for some Bible reading. He reckoned it might provide comfort at the least and might even serve to uplift the spirits of his wife and their offspring.

Father and mother sat in their usual chairs, near the fireplace that lay empty and unused. The children formed a semi-circle around their parents on the floor. Isaiah and Margaret took turns reading passes from the Good Book. She preferred the Psalms and read several of them. Isaiah chose the New Testament. He read with great feeling and great volume. So loud, that the family could hear nothing inside, or outside, their wooden home.

It was during the reading of a passage from the Book of Revelation that the front door burst open, forced by a howling and forceful west wind. A supernova of brightness flooded into the candle-lit sitting room. A wave of hot, smoky air blew into the house.

Isaiah dropped his Bible and ran to the front door, curious at the sound and the fury that had interrupted his family's prayers. When he reached the now-open doorway, he saw the impending firewall.

"My God, My God, why have you abandoned me?" he quoted from Scripture.

In another instant, the flames lashed out at the farmhouse. Before any of the Hills could move to safety, the blaze surrounded and consumed the family dwelling. The roof caved in, crushing all ten of the family members. Most died in their prayer places, Margaret in her chair and the children on the floor. Isaiah Hill was blown back by the ferocious wind against the rear wall of the parlor. His body landed in a crumpled heap on the floor just as the burning wooden shingles from the roof rained down upon him.

The Hill farmhouse burned to the foundation within a matter of minutes. All that remained were the fireplace and chimney in the sitting room and the kitchen cook stove, which melted somewhat but did not move.

*   *   *

Back in the town center, Father Peter Pernin was unable to see his unfinished church from the Peshtigo River. But if he had, his faith and hope might have been dashed.

Blowing ferociously from the west, part of the Great Peshtigo fireball rumbled to the corner of Oconto and Ellis Avenues, near where the Catholic house of worship was being built. Within seconds, the wind slammed the accompanying flames straight through the unfinished structure. The fire consumed the wooden frame almost instantly. Fed by the flooring and sides of the building, the flames raced upward, climbing and then enshrouding the church steeple. After destroying the wood, the inferno attacked the metal bell. The sheer size of the fire and its extraordinary heat hurled the bell from its tower to the ground below. The molten metal hit the ground so hard, the bell buried itself several feet into the charred ground.

What had taken Father Pernin and his parishioners months to build was reduced to rubble and ashes within minutes.

The calamitous fire expanded in size and severity as it came into contact with the buildings in central Peshtigo. The fearsome winds kept it moving quickly. The blaze outran many people trying to escape from it.

There were two hundred men staying at the Jacobs Hotel, most of whom had just arrived from abroad for the coming lumber-harvesting season. They were Germans, Irish, Scandinavians, and French-Canadians. Some spoke no English. Most had no idea the drought had been so severe. The hotel patrons were involved in their own pursuits that Sunday night. Many were enjoying supper in the dining room. Others had just finished and were in their rooms preparing to sleep. Several were in the Jacobs bar, having a nightcap before calling it a day.

The well-fed fire was now spurting flames some sixty feet skyward. It was several blocks wide. It was moving faster than a hurricane or tornado but its noise sounded like both of those phenomena in one. And yet, in the din of the Jacobs Hotel, few heard the blaze as it roared into the building. It attacked the multi-story hotel with no mercy. The front porch disintegrated, the walls burst into flames, curtains and carpets ignited, windows exploded, spewing shards of glass which slashed several men.

The flames blew sparks in all directions, burning other nearby structures. The smoke became so thick, people inside could not see, nor could they breathe. Many died from asphyxiation, before they could even move to escape. Others were burned alive. No one escaped. The catastrophic fire moved from building to building, reducing everything in its path to rubble.

Just north of Peshtigo, offshoots of the main fire imperiled farms, fields, and forests. In the heat of the night, three farm families came together, seeking survival from the cataclysm. By some stroke of luck James Johnston had decided to plow under his corn crop just a week earlier. The stalks had withered and died. The mere sight of the failed crop angered and distressed Johnston so he assembled his team of horses, attached his trusty plow, and walked for two days through his fallow field in the heat and haze. Most of the stalks had been covered by the dirt.

When the wildfire blew toward their farms, James and two neighbor families came to the same hasty conclusion: they had no ponds or streams nearby, so it would be safer to be in a dirt field when the flames tore through than it was to be in a house, a barn, or near the wooded sections of their property.

With little time to spare, Hiram Paulding and Matthew Polk herded their wives and children to the Johnston corn field. Their arrival coincided with a decision by James to bring his own family out into the field. Twenty-four men, women, and children now congregated nervously in the center of that field. The men conferred quickly and formulated a plan. The three women and the older children would lie down first, then the younger ones would lie on top of them. They would be covered by the blankets and quilts the families had brought for warmth against the night chill. The men realized the extraordinary heat would eliminate the night chill instantly. They realized too that the heat would smother those under the blankets.

So James Johnston and Hiram Paulding ran to the Johnston farm house, some two hundred yards away. The men retrieved four buckets of water. They hurried back to their assembled and frightened families.

Time had run out. The blaze was approaching. It was attacking the trees and bushes that surrounded the plowed corn field. The men draped the covers over the women and children and proceeded to douse them with all the water they had.

The fire lunged across the field like a gigantic ocean wave crashing to the shore in a tropical storm. The men emptied their pails. Because the wind was gusting so fiercely, they lay down upon their families to prevent the blankets and quilts from blowing aside, which the men knew would mean certain death for the mothers and their children.

The swift-charging inferno took several minutes to scorch the entire farm field and move on. Its next target was James Johnston's home and barn. As the flames shot through the house, the heat's combustion caused a massive blast inside the wooden structure. It blew the home's huge metal stove twenty feet into the air. The stove landed on top of the water well, smashing the stone sides of the well to pebbles. The fire howled as it consumed the home and barn, emitting a piercing sound like a siren screeching through the darkness of a damp night.

In the field, when the conflagration had passed by and the air above her blanket cooled somewhat, Sally Polk squirmed. She removed her daughter who'd been lying on her, stomach pressed hard into her mother's back. Sally eased herself out from under the cover. She first noticed that the blanket was singed and blackened by the fire. But it had withstood the fiery onslaught.

Then she made her first grim discovery. All three men were dead. They lay in crumpled heaps at the edge of the covered group. Much of the men's clothing had been burned away and reduced to ash. Their skin was charred and dotted with heat bubbles. They looked like animals just removed from an outside cooking spit. The faces of all three were frozen in terror. But Sally Polk could not recall the men making any sounds as the inferno blew over them.

Sally could not bear to look at them. She prayed that their suffering had been minimal, that their deaths had come quickly. And then she feared that some of the twenty other women and children had been burned alive along with the men.

"The fire has passed," she said in slightly hushed tones. "You can come out now."

Slowly, the quilts and blankets were thrust aside. The two other mothers looked around and screamed at the horrific site next to them. Their brave husbands were gone. All three women took the blankets and covered the men so the children would be spared the protracted view of their fathers' battered and burned bodies.

To the women's amazement, all eighteen children had survived. They had been saved by James Johnston, Hiram Paulding, and Matthew Polk and their quick action to moisten the blankets, cover their kin, lie atop their wives, and save the lives of their families.

The twenty-one survivors held hands. Sally Polk led them in a prayer. They thanked God for their salvation from the flames and they commended the souls of three good men to heaven.

Peshtigo

Then they all stood and moved away from the dead men. Burials could come in the morning but not now. In the dark, the women did not know where to go and they could not see very far. But they could clearly smell the stench of burnt vegetation all around them. And, too, there was the smell of death.

At last, Amanda Johnston suggested the three families should walk several paces from the men's bodies, stop and sit in a group, get some rest, and wait until morning when they could better assess the damage.

"We have no doubt lost everything," Amanda said. "But at least we twenty-one are alive."

* * *

By far the largest structure in the town was the Peshtigo Company mill and factory. The building was nearly a block long and it was made completely from wood. All around it lay mountains of logs and planks. Some of them were to be milled and sent south. Some were to be made into boards for construction of new homes and businesses in this region and in the city of Green Bay. And some were to be carried inside the woodenware plant and made into the barrels, buckets, broom handles, and clothes pegs. Of course, there were also by-products of all this output: wood chips and sawdust collected in mountainous piles around the huge building, stretching down toward the Peshtigo River.

And, as it marched from west to east, the firestorm eventually reached the mammoth structure. There was so much fodder for the fire that it became more like an unchained erupting volcano. Flames first shot upward, pushing sparks, ash, soot, and pieces of unburned wood deep into the night sky. Then the blaze exploded outward in rapid-fire bursts. People rushing past the factory toward the river were blown down by the force of the thermal explosions. Some died immediately, dropping limply onto the dirt street or wooden sidewalks. Others were felled by fiery flying projectiles, which severed arms and legs or blew away heads and torsos. Broom handles acted like burning spears sailing through the air. Those struck by them died instantly. Flaming chunks of buckets smashed into people. One hit a young child in the head, setting her on fire.

127

She died before her father could put out the flames or remove the bucket from her body.

The forcefulness of the fire also sent flames shooting sideways, toward the river itself and even across it. A sheet of flame fell onto a crowd taking cover in the water. It was so severe that even dropping below the surface couldn't save them. Some burned to death, while others drowned as they attempted to stay under water until the flames subsided. The burning dust and debris that was catapulted across the water set new ground ablaze. The fire consumed the desiccated grass and flower beds, then raced to the first set of homes of the eastern bank of the Peshtigo.

The flaming catastrophe knocked down much of the Peshtigo Company complex but because of its sheer size, the building burned for hours. Some cinder block walls withstood the onslaught. Everything else was destroyed.

*   *   *

The collapse of the bridge and the destruction of the warehouse sent additional pieces of wood careening into the river. The hundreds who had sought shelter in the warm but moist refuge were gripped with a new terror. Fiery logs came at them like torpedoes from a submarine. As they scrambled to evade them, the refugees slammed into one another or trampled those who had gone under the water to escape the heat. And there was another challenge. Animals had rushed to the water just as humans had. Their instincts told them the river would protect them.

Dogs, horses, cows, and goats clawed for safety above and below the water line. Most of the animals were terror-stricken. Their movements were erratic, frightened. As some of the larger animals thrashed and pushed, they struck people trying to hold their place in the riverbed. The frail humans proved no contest to the equine and bovine onslaught. Several people were trampled to death, others were drowned as the animals pinned people underwater.

*   *   *

Peshtigo

The Great Peshtigo Fire destroyed more than a town, it devastated an entire region of Northern Wisconsin and Northwestern Michigan. But the human toll of the catastrophe made it so appalling. J.E. Beebe worked in the Peshtigo Company's mill. His task was to make sure the huge logs that were brought to the mill got on the massive conveyor belt and were then cut into boards. It was a hard job but a rewarding one. He loved it. And the weekly wage paid for his home, fed himself, his wife, and their four children, and made him quite content.

But as he and his family took flight on this October Sunday night, they opted for the safety of the river, just as so many other Peshtigans were doing.

All six members of the Beebe clan rushed for the water. They encountered great crowds of others fleeing the fire. They tried to push their way through the mass of people and animals. Somehow, in the confusion of their flight, all six family members became separated. The parents began a frantic search for the children, even as scores of their neighbors hurried past to the river's edge. Three of the children stopped running and they began looking for their father and mother. But four-year-old Alexandra had no qualms about the dissociation with other family members. She continued jogging, pushed along by the huge crowd, toward the river.

Several blocks away, the spitting, sputtering fire roared through the area, devouring homes and shops and barns with a sickening and insatiable appetite. The Beebe family, still intent on finding one another, paid more attention to their search than to their approaching doom. The huge fire became their funeral pyre. The flames struck down J.E. Beebe, his wife Essie, and three of their children. As they lay dead in the darkened and scorched street, Alexandra Beebe reached the Peshtigo River. She did not know that she had become an orphan. But she somehow understood that she'd be safer in the water than running through the streets or stopping to look for her family. As she watched others bobbing in and out of the water to moisten their skin and their clothing, Alexandra did likewise. Her fear at being alone was overcome by the certainty that she was safe and that when the morning sun rose, she would find her mother, father, brothers and sister. Now all she had to do was stay cool and stay wet. And there was one other task. Just before the fire reached the river, it was preceded by tornado-like wind gusts. They were so potent they knocked children like Alexandra Beebe backward as they stood on the river bottom. So the little girl decided to twist her shoes deeper into the river-bottom mud. This would anchor her, she thought, and help her maintain her footing.

*   *   *

After decimating the Peshtigo bridge, the conflagration charged the east bank of the river, maintaining its sound and fury. The wind rebuilt its momentum, howling at the same speed and with the same fury as on the western side of the town. The flames remained ferocious. The drifting smoke was just as thick. It had passed over the river, unaffected by the water.

It was not long before the rejuvenated fire found a large new target. It attacked a three-story Boarding House, actually surrounding the wooden building with flames, smoke, flying embers, and immense heat. It danced from the lobby to each of the rooms. The occupants of the Boarding House had no chance to escape. Other flames shot up the walls, straining to reach the roof.

In less than five minutes, the dry wood was destroyed and the building collapsed in a burning heap. The screams from inside the Boarding House could no longer be heard. The sixty people inside had died horrible deaths. Ten of them were local residents, working at the facility.

All the rest were Norwegian immigrants who had just arrived in Wisconsin to start anew and, they had hoped, find better lives in America.

*   *   *

The monster made its way through the rest of Peshtigo. Virtually everything in its path was reduced to ash. The most deadly and devastating fire the United States has ever known affected the lives of all two thousand people who called Peshtigo home. Just two structures survived the fiery offensive: A small house at the western edge of the town, on the Charles Schwartz farm, had somehow been spared. Everything around it was charred beyond recognition.

Peshtigo

On the eastern side of Peshtigo, an unfinished house was untouched although other houses in the vicinity were obliterated. The structure was being built as the future home of a superintendent at the Peshtigo Company. Carpenters had scooped out the earth for the basement and had just laid the wood flooring. That's as far as they got when the fire roared through. The owner of the house had purchased newer and greener wood from the company store and it may have acted as a fire retardant.

The death toll was catastrophic. But there were scores of survivors. As they hid in the heat-warmed water of the river, or other refuges, many commented on the spectacle that overwhelmed and nearly overpowered them.

One survivor called it "a towering wall of fire, higher than Niagara, rolling over everything in its path."

To others it was "a solid wall of fire", "a waterfall of fire rolling and tumbling".

Still others described what they saw as an "avalanche of fire", "a river of fire", and "Great balls of fire like flaming missiles shot from unseen artillery".

A woman who had narrowly escaped from the west bank conflagration watched as the Peshtigo Company burned to the ground. She noticed that "in seconds, the pine sidewalls were afire. Then the dry sawdust around the factory and in the streets mushroomed into flame."

The unprecedented inferno was not only potent, it was also fast. At 8:30 p.m., residents first noticed the unholy glow in the Southwestern sky that signaled the approach of the killer fire. An hour later, people were still lunging for the Peshtigo River, leaping to safety in the water as the fire aimed its destruction at the waterway. By 10 p.m., the town was in a state of panic because the blaze had destroyed much of the western part of Peshtigo and was leveling important landmarks like the company sawmill. By 10:30, cataclysm. The entire village was destroyed. The fire moved on.

After laying waste to the community, the blaze rampaged through the countryside, pushing its way to Marinette and Menominee, six miles from Peshtigo, on the Menominee River, one town in Wisconsin, the other in Michigan. But as it bore down on the twin towns, the wind-whipped flames sought new targets to destroy. As the flames licked their way through Northern Wisconsin, they lapped up acre after acre of wild lands and tree after tree. The fire obliterated many of the sixty logging and lumber camps. Perhaps most remarkable was the path of the fire. Flames grabbed trees by the trunk and the wind pushed flames up the trees and into their foliage. Then the wind's force caused flames to erupt several feet above the tree itself. Smoldering embers hurled off the burning brush might set a neighboring tree alight. But at the very same time, the fire would burn downward, attacking the roots of the trees, deep into the earth. The inferno spread below ground as well as above it.

As the fire spread northward, residents of Menominee and Marinette caught a series of natural breaks. They were close to water, on the Menominee River and not far from the Green Bay. The river protected the villages on one side, the Bay acted as a buffer on the other. But the two towns also benefitted from a stretch of sandy hills, some forty to fifty feet high. Deposited by an ancient glacier, the hills created a barrier which prevented the fire from progressing. These slowed its fiery pace, reduced its ferocity, and forced the flames to divide. When it split in two directions, the blaze lost some of its punch and veered away from the two towns. Menominee and Marinette each had populations of more than two thousand.

While one wing of the fire veered to the north and west, aiming for remote regions of Wisconsin and Michigan, the second stream took dead aim at Menekaune, a neighborhood of Marinette.

One resident ran through the streets alerting townspeople to seek safe haven.

"The fire is approaching the area with the speed of a race horse," the sentinel told one worried resident.

People once again ran for the river, this time the Menominee. Some waded in but others boarded the three steamers that were anchored at the town's port. Women and children were piled onto the Union, the George L. Dunlap, and the St. Joseph. All three soon filled with occupants, then shoved off from the pier, and became floating evacuation sites in the middle of the wide waterway. The captains of the three craft conferred and decided to move their vessels out into Green Bay for additional safety.

Peshtigo

Men, unable to board the steamers, covered themselves with the cold waters of the river as the fire bore down on Menekaune.

At the Marinette shipyard, owner S.V.D Philbrook called several men, women, and children who were dashing toward the river. He told them to board his schooner, called the Stella. When the ship was filled to capacity, Philbrook hoisted the ropes and let the Stella drift out into the river. Within a few minutes, the schooner clipped a sandbar and became stuck. The boat had grounded itself. This caused momentary panic aboard the vessel. But Captain Philbrook appealed for calm, suggesting the vessel was far enough into the river to avoid the dangers of the approaching blaze.

The remnants of the Great Peshtigo fire barreled into Menekaune. It gained new force and speed as it was refueled by wooden structures in the area. The blaze consumed thirty-five homes, ten barns, three shops, two hotels, a pair of sawmills, a door factory, and several farm animals. But not a single person died. Their hasty evacuation had saved them.

Even though the winds blew the fire away from the center of Marinette, its sheer strength still led to destruction there. Fourteen buildings were fire victims, including a mill, a boarding house, and a factory.

And despite its seeming protection by bodies of water, the flames managed to leap the river and roar into Menoninee itself. A mill and several houses were burned to the ground. And because many in the town felt the water would insulate them from the fire, they took no precautions. A handful of the town's citizens were killed.

By midnight of that fateful October day, the fearsome fire had passed through Marinette and Menominee. It faltered a bit but continued its path of destruction. It struck just one more town before burning itself out in Michigan's Upper Peninsula.

That community, Birch Creek, had a population of about one hundred people. They had no warning of the fire's fast approach. It steamed through the tiny town, sending most of the buildings up in flames and smoke.

Twenty-two residents died. They were the last victims of the Great Peshtigo conflagration.

Chapter 9

As the western side of Wisconsin's Green Bay was being destroyed by a calamitous firestorm, the waterway's eastern flank was being attacked by its own fire disaster. It began just a few miles north and east of the city of Green Bay but citizens of northern Wisconsin's largest community knew nothing of the infernos raging on each side of the Bay. Green Bay slept through the worst fire in United States history.

Still, the fires blazed on. Their initial target was the town of New Franken, twelve miles from Green Bay. In the approaching darkness that fateful Sunday evening a ghastly combination developed: A deafening sound, caused by a wind propelled from the southwest, then fire balls floating through the night, raining flames and hot embers down on pines and oaks and maples and dried grass. The more it consumed, the hotter the inferno became. As it gained strength, the blaze gave off toxic gasses even hotter than the main fire line. And it produced thick, heavy smoke that choked animals and gagged humans. It was a duplicate of the deadly conflagration that ruined Peshtigo and other towns on the Bay's western shore.

The wind-whipped barrage first attacked a log barn and cottage near New Franken and these acted as kindling, giving the fire new potency and a bigger appetite. It lunged for a massive wood pile, where three thousand cords of wood were stored. The fire erupted, flames streaming hundreds of feet into the night sky which turned darkness into light. Pieces of wood acted as rockets, pushed skyward and projected like shrapnel in every direction surrounding the pyre.

Several of those burning bits slammed into the nearby saw mill which had created the lumber pile. The resulting explosion startled people for miles. They left their homes hastily and began running, not knowing where to go or where to hide.

The conflagration now created a chain reaction. As one structure caught fire, it spewed sparks toward the next targets. There was almost no time to react or take preventive measures.

Five houses on the edge of New Franken were set aflame next. As usual, all were of wooden construction from roof to floor. They were reduced to ash within minutes. A wooden sidewalk in the front of the obliterated homes went next. It acted as if it were a long fuse leading to some distant sticks of dynamite. The blaze raced along the walkway and into the center of the village. It stopped at nothing, growing more ravenous as it reached another home, shop, or barn.

East of the village center, the main fire ignited a major grassfire and it barreled toward a series of farms and barns. It spread to a width of three miles, a blazing tsunami some twenty feet high. Given its size, its depth, and its intensity, the firestorm attacked and leveled everything in its path. In one fiery gulp, it attacked three farmhouses and two barns simultaneously. Two families managed to flee their homes, racing for a nearly dry pond between the two properties. The third family never got off the farmhouse's front porch. Five of them were felled by the force of the flames. As the fire danced over their bodies, charring them, the smell of burnt flesh now joined the ashy odor of destroyed wood.

New Franken residents had scurried out of their homes when they heard the sound of the fury.

As they ran for safety, many saw the unstoppable inferno. They described "balls of fire" and "fire flakes" and even "fire balloons" and the deafening sound was likened to hurricanes, cyclones, and tornadoes.

One group of residents reached the community school house and pulled open the unlocked door. There were about a dozen of them.

"Get under desks, chairs, in cupboards, any place that will provide more protection," said one man to the crowd almost divided evenly between men and women. It was a catastrophic mistake.

They barely had time to reach cover before the flames roared over the school, engulfing much of it. Windows cracked or were blown inward, sending shards of glass flying toward the crouching asylum-seekers. The heat melted curtains, blackboards and books on the single classroom's book shelves. The flames had scaled the walls and roared across the structure's roof. In no time, sections of the roof caved in, hurling sparks and debris across the classroom. The walls tumbled next but they fell outward. Desks burned quickly. Metal legs began melting in the grotesque heat. The floor caught fire and crackled and the blaze gnawed its way through thick floor boards. Then the brightness of the flames subsided, the heat cooled somewhat, and all was still. The conflagration had moved on. For many moments, there was no sound, no movement.

In time, a seventy-six-year-old grandmother thanked God her prayers for deliverance had been answered. She then moved a slightly charred board that has fallen across her legs and she crawled out from under the teacher's desk, which had been her hiding place.

"I am unhurt," she spoke toward the center of the darkened and heavily damaged school room. "You can come out now. The fire has moved on. Is anyone hurt?'

But there was no response; indeed, there was no sound. The others lay dead, killed by asphyxiation or the fire itself. One woman near the center of the school house was crushed when a piece of the roof rained down on her.

The elderly lady searched the rubble and confirmed that the others were gone. Then she dropped to the charred floor, began weeping, and spoke out loud.

"Oh God, you have spared me, an old woman with my days fulfilled but you have taken my sons and my daughters from me," she sobbed in her prayer of thanksgiving and of simultaneous despair.

Across New Franken, terrified townspeople evacuated their homes, with little thought about where to seek safety. Some streaked for water. Some ran to basements, root cellars, and wells. A few ran to the stone church near the edge of the village, reasoning the fire could not penetrate the heavy stone walls.

But the blaze shot upward in the howling wind, then dropped from the heavens like some atomic bomb. It rained fire, gas, ash, and smoke across the town. The flames destroyed buildings, the logs brought to town for milling, piles of sawdust and tailings heaped near the mill and at the edges of the community.

The Great Eastern Bay fire moved through New Franken at eight miles per hour. It leveled every building in town, even the stone church was weakened by the fire and toppled by the wind. Many of the residents who made it to water survived. A few died in their shelters. One child who took shelter in a well not only suffocated but was roasted from the extraordinary heat. A husband and wife were incinerated in a root cellar. All the fruits and vegetables were nothing but blackened cinders.

Peshtigo

After the firewall charged through the town, it was blown northeastward by the sirocco. The survivors began to gather near the town center to discuss their good fortune and their losses. As they looked around, they saw only destruction. Then farmer Michael Hime raced into the village from the countryside.

"The woods and the heavens were all on fire," he reported to the assembled crowd. "But I am shocked at what has happened here."

Abner Willcox, who lived in New Franken, merely nodded.

"The fire rose up several feet, perhaps fifty feet above the tree tops," he recounted. "Then it would leap across fields and yards, burning everything. Finally it flamed up into the forest and blew on. It was the most frightening sight of my life."

"I could not believe the overpowering roar of the wind," Thelma Rose said, still seeming nervous and unsteady. "It knocked me down as I tried to run for shelter. Thank God I was able to get to my feet and reach the creek."

One man joined the small throng.

"I have just carried this torch with me around the village. My house is destroyed, my family is missing. In fact, every house is gone, as is every barn. There is no evidence New Franken ever existed."

*   *   *

The nightmare that ruined New Franken was about to begin farther up the peninsula.

In the small town of Rosiere the residents had many things in common. Nearly all of them had come to Wisconsin from Belgium. They had similar upbringing, similar customs and similar traditions.

They brought their Old World ways to their New world and they followed certain traditions as they left their homeland. When they arrived in the Upper Midwest, they gravitated to Rosiere, following other Belgians who had preceded them. The earliest pioneers among them had settled the town, then written home to tell friends about the riches of this region, its vast forests, its fertile and level fields for farming, its normally clean and crisp weather, its religious freedoms.

The newcomers followed a familiar path and chose to farm the land. And because they had enjoyed Belgian beer back home, the transplants grew the grains needed to make the delectable brew. While the men tilled the fields with their hands, the women were artisans with their hands, many associated with a thriving textile trade back home. Once they had settled in Wisconsin, the women made clothing, quilts, even American versions of prized Belgian lace.

Life was so good that more people ventured on ships from Antwerp to New York, then overland to Chicago, Milwaukee, and finally the Green Bay peninsula. Not wanting to cram themselves close together in these wide open spaces, the Belgians eventually moved beyond Rosiere to other existing communities or they built new towns which they incorporated themselves. They settled in places like Forestville and Union. And one group called their new community Brussels, as most of the new Wisconsinites had come from the area around Belgium's capital city.

Most were farmers and a few were loggers but other Belgians opened shops to serve their fellow countrymen and women. Charles Rubens ran the General Store in Rosiere. He offered his friends and neighbors the basic foodstuffs and household needs. But on rare occasions he sold specialities from back home. Textiles were the easiest to ship so they were abundant on his store shelves. He'd had some success importing bottles of Belgian beer, although many bottles broke during the arduous sea and land journey from home. And one time, a member of his wife's family carried five boxes of Belgian chocolate back from a trip to visit relatives near Bruges. More than half melted or lost its deep dark coloring. Charles was able to sell individual pieces of the candy from the nearly two boxes that survived the five-thousand-mile voyage. Customers paid well for the treats and told Charles later how delicious the chocolates had been. The Rubens family ate a few pieces from a third box and found the product palatable but hardly as delicious as the rich, creamy chocolate served in shops of Brussels and Bruges. His customers told Charles they enjoyed having the treat from their homeland and they were grateful he had managed to get some shipped to Wisconsin.

Peshtigo

Charles Rubens was married to Cherie, the daughter of a Belgian cloth tradesman, who had opposed the decision by his daughter and son-in-law to leave their native land and embark on a dangerous trip to the darkest regions of the upper Midwest of the United States. But as Charles prospered in his new land, Cherie's parents came to respect the couple for its successes.

The Rubens had six children, stretching in ages from twelve to two. There were four girls, the two oldest and the two youngest of the children. The boys came in the middle. Every one of the children, except the baby Madeleine, had chores both at home and at the Rubens store. And over the last several weeks, the children and their parents had taken on another responsibility: evacuation and refuge drills in case of fire.

Now on this warm Sunday night in October, as the sun vanished in the Western sky, the family finished a light supper, cleared away after the meal, and embarked on quiet time for reading and knitting.

It was not long before the rumbling began, low and sullen at first, then deafening and threatening. Charles rose from his sitting room chair and pulled open his heavy wooden front door. Brightness simulating high noon poured through the front door, vanquishing the darkness. Flames licked at the trees off in the southwest, then shot upward from the fuel of dead limbs and leaves. Searing heat pushed its way toward the Rubens front door, forcing Charles back from the doorway.

"Everyone!" he yelled. "It is a fire. We must begin our escape plan."

No one hesitated. They hastened to grab blankets and coats and headed quickly for the rear of the house. They moved quietly and if anyone were frightened, no one showed any outward signs. Their training had taken them to a well pit that had gone dry. A ladder had been dropped into the well. Charles helped his wife descend first. She also carried a candle and wooden matches. Once at the bottom, she would light the candle, then provide comfort and solace to her children as they climbed down into the near darkness. Charles lifted each child to the top rungs of the ladder, guiding them down the steps until they were out of his reach. When all six were out of sight, he mounted the ladder and lowered himself below ground level.

But when he reached the bottom, crowded tightly with the remainder of his family, Charles Rubens became almost immediately overheated, claustrophobic, and immensely scared.

The heat became more acute with each second, as the potent fire pushed closer to the Rubens property. Ahead of the fiery storm, smoke billowed across the land, then discovered the well opening, and drifted down to coat the family.

Just as his wife began to panic, Charles Rubens knew he had to relocate his family, and fast.

"Children, Mother," he said as calmly as he could muster, "we must leave this pit now. I fear the fire is too big. The heat and smoke will harm us here."

Without further words, he hustled up the ladder, then turned.

"Children, come up quickly."

One by one, the half-dozen Rubens offspring climbed back out of the empty well. Finally, Cherie brought up the rear.

"Follow me!" he commanded.

Holding hands, the eight of them sprinted for open fields upwind. Charles felt their only chance was to get out of the line of fire. It would work only if the wind maintained its present course.

The spewing inferno was bearing down on their house and their well. The Rubens clan ran until all the family members heard the detonation.

Thermal combustion blew the house apart, precipitating billows of flame and smoke. The intensity of the explosion changed the direction of the wind. It was now heading straight for the family. Charles stopped running, huddled his frightened and weary family together, then ordered everyone to drop to the ground.

The mean fire roared toward them but at the last moment, the southwest wind regained its strength and blew the fire in the northeasterly direction it had been traveling since coming to life back near New Franken.

This occurred so suddenly that none of the family members had time to cover up with the blankets or coats they had brought for protection. In fact, Cherie had scampered up the ladder so quickly, she had left her blanket at the base of the well pit.

Even several yards away, the fire affected the entire Rubens family in a very few minutes. The heat left skin burns, the kind a full day in the hot sun generally produced.

The piercing smoke had gagged all of them. They coughed and wheezed until the fire had passed by and clearer air followed. A few of the children went momentarily deaf from the cyclonic sound of the raging forest fire. Cherie was blinded for a moment, having peered at the blaze at the moment it was highest and closest to them.

But miraculously, they were all safe. No one moved until the cool of the night air enveloped them completely. Charles stood first. He lent a hand to his wife, who stood next to him. The two adults then went to the children, inspecting each to make certain they were not injured seriously.

"Merci bien, mon Dieu," Charles uttered in his native French. As the family marched slowly back toward their charred home, all of them spoke the Lord's Prayer in unison in French. It was their familial prayer of thanksgiving.

Before reaching the house, they paused at the well pit. Charles descended once more to retrieve the candle and the blanket left behind by Cherie. He knew there would be little to salvage from the house and the candle might be the only source of light to help them see their way across their field.

When he returned to the surface, Charles showed each of them the blanket. It was charred and torn into bits. He told them the candle had been melted and the wooden matches ignited from the intensity of the rising heat level in the confined space of the pit.

"Had we stayed down there, I am certain we would have perished."

Two of the girls began to cry but their mother hushed and comforted them.

"Our house appears to be destroyed," said Charles. "I can only guess the shop has been damaged but there is little or nothing we can do in the darkness. Let us go near the garden, put down the blankets and coats we have, and get some rest. We will take stock when the sun comes up."

The Rubens family was one of the luckiest in Rosiere. The firestorm pillaged the town, destroying nearly every home and barn and store.

Forty-four Belgians who had come to this part of the world for a better life, lost their lives in the heat, fire, and smoke of the awful blaze.

And as the fire continued on its destructive path, it leveled many neighboring communities. Nearly forty people perished in Forestville. Others died in Union and Brussels. Most of the dead were immigrants, who spoke little or no English and who had thought that such tragedies could never befall this most blessed of lands, steeped in natural beauty and abundant in natural resources. But in a matter of moments, the newcomers' heaven-on-earth had become hell.

* * *

As with the series of fires on the western front of the Green Bay, the eastern blazes created their own nefarious feeding frenzy. As the flames gobbled up wooden structures, desiccated trees, and bone-dry grassland, the fires grew exponentially. Sparks and embers rocketed high into the sky, coming down hot on other objects and bursting into new flame. When homes were engulfed, the blaze became so hot it appeared to expel so-called fire balloons from the doomed structures. When these burst, they made a horrendous situation far worse.

In point of fact, several of these balloons of fire were carried in an easterly direction by the locomotive-sounding, omnipotent wind, after the flames had ravaged the village of Union. The incredibly hot bubbles drifted upward, aided by the wind. As they came into contact with cooler air aloft, the balloons burst, shooting superheated shards back down to earth. Some fell on the dry ground of the eastern shore of the peninsula, fanning more fires. Some fell into Lake Michigan, setting even parts of the massive waterway ablaze temporarily. And other gaseous fragments cascaded down onto an island half a mile offshore. The drought-dried grasses and foliage on the uninhabited land mass burst into flames. They were not extinguished until the fire had blackened the entire island and slipped over the edges into the cool waters of the Great Lake.

* * *

Peshtigo bore the flaming brunt of the destruction on the west side of Green Bay. On the eastern peninsula, that dubious distinction fell to Williamsonville. Situated on the water, the small town had prospered in the years since being founded by the Williamson brothers.

By the October night of the inferno, it was a small but tight-knit community of seventy-six people, forty-five men, fifteen women, and sixteen children. Lumber was king here. Nearly every man was involved in milling the logs carried in by horse or floated in by barge. The Williamsonville brothers' operation had been very productive and the village's success was evident. Piles of lumber, awaiting shipment downstate, small heaps of unprocessed logs, and mountains of wood chips and wood dust were omnipresent.

The drought of 1871 had slowed the timber business. But all the residents of Williamsonville felt it was a temporary setback and that business would be back to normal by winter, when rain and snow would return to their rightful place in northern Wisconsin.

Still, the women were fearful of the dry conditions. Most of the married men were concerned as well. But the single workers who relied on work to give meaning to their lives ignored the harsh realities, planned on returning to work Monday, and dreamed of many good days to come.

On this Sunday, it was quiet in Williamsonville just after dark. Townspeople were preparing for another hot, dry, still, and sleepless night. But in an instant, the soporific tone throughout the town gave way to an attitude charged with electricity and with emotion.

A sound like a tornado signaled the approach of ferocious winds. It was that overwhelming noise which rousted the local residents from their beds and their homes. On the heals of the zephyr came the increasing light, brightening quickly and overwhelmingly like the shock of an atomic blast some eighty years later. At the town center, the sight of the blaze made men sweat, women and children scream in terror. The fire seemed as high as Niagara Falls, spewing sparks and embers, spreading unbelievable heat and smoke as it roamed freely toward the tiny community.

The disbelieving citizens were stunned by what they saw, almost frozen in place. Then they began running for open space. Their goal was a potato patch at the village edge.

A young girl panicked and did not keep up. When the fire reached the child, her clothing burned instantly. A mill hand who saw it but could do nothing to save her said of the girl, "she burned like a swift candle".

Because the wind had been blowing for so long its velocity had become overwhelming. It pushed the fire quickly into Williamsonville, even before some residents could escape. It attacked men, women, and children, mowing them down with the force of a cyclone. Flames rushed from body to body. Flesh crackled in the unrelenting heat.

Two people rushing for the open space of the potato field were trapped when a huge pine tree, covered in flames, fell over on them. Rescuers who found the man's and woman's body some days later were not sure whether they were crushed to death by the tree trunk, which was some forty inches in circumference, or whether they had survived the tree but burned to death.

The storm of fire turned its savagery on the homes and stores of the small town. As with many communities before it, the structures in Williamsonville caught fire and were destroyed in a matter of minutes. And when the violence of the blaze reached the local sawmill, it struck the jackpot.

The flames were all-encompassing, so intense that the large building toppled quickly, flamed out, and then smoldered for days.

Of the seventy-six citizens who lived in Williamsonville, seventeen survived the fury but the victims were found in two areas. Twenty-four residents, including the man and woman killed by the tree and the young girl whose clothes caught fire, died in the village proper. And there was a twelve-year-old boy who split from his family as it sought safety in the open space beyond the town. The child doubted he could run all the way to the potato field, so he jumped into an outdoor cooking oven behind the home of a neighbor. He pulled shut the metal door and figured the stone and steel which now surrounded him would also save him. But the massive blaze that blew through Williamsonville surrounded the oven, after consuming the adjacent wooden home, and heated stones to unbearable levels.

The fire surrounded the oven, after consuming the adjacent wooden home and heated the stones to unbearable levels. The boy's suffering may have seemed interminable but in reality it took the fire only a few minutes to roast the boy alive.

The other thirty-five died in the potato field. They had gambled that a large open dirt field might retard the fire's potency and prevent its spread. They were wrong. Their bodies lay twisted in grotesque shapes and angles. The grimaces on the faces suggested the utter agony they must have suffered before dying. Many bodies were incomplete. The skin had burned away from bones leaving ashes and blackened chunks of flesh in small heaps. Near some corpses were earrings, rings, a pocket watch. For those charred beyond recognition, it would be the only way recovery teams would identify those taken by the wrath of the fire.

The survivors benefited from good fortune. They managed to run away from the fire's destructive path or hide where the furious fire couldn't reach them. They prayed and sobbed and comforted one another for being spared when so many of their friends and neighbors were not.

Aside from the human loss, Williamsonville lost every building to the fire. Even the town dock, which held the ships bringing in supplies and taking wood products out of town, was burnt to cinders, and some charred pieces of the dock floated out into the Green Bay. With most of its people gone and its structures decimated, Williamsonville would cease to be. It never rebuilt.

The firestorm continued its deadly and destructive march to the north but just northeast of Williamsonville the winds swirled around forcing the leading edge of the fire back against itself. The inferno was now fighting fire with fire, similar to what forest firefighters do in modern times, create a burn-line to retard a fire's forward progress. It caused the tempest to taper off. With no propelling force, the fire stood still and burned itself down. It stopped short of the town of Sturgeon Bay. But these blazes had consumed virtually all of the Green Bay's eastern peninsula from New Franken to beyond Williamsonville.

In some two hours on the night of October 8, 1871, the most deadly fire in United States history and perhaps the single worst natural calamity ever to strike North America wrecked more than three and three-quarter million acres of forests, farmland, and population centers. The human death toll would never be certain but more than eighteen hundred people perished. Thousands of animals were snuffed out. The damage to the region as well as its economy was inestimable. Yet no one outside the battered region were even aware of the immense tragedy. The rest of the world would not know about it for days.

What came to be known as the Great Peshtigo Fire would be overshadowed by another raging inferno more than two hundred miles to the south.

The Great Chicago Fire was burning at exactly the same time as the Peshtigo megafire.

From its source on the city's South Side the Great Calamity, as many referred to it, burned some four-and-a-half miles of urban landscape. It stopped only upon reaching the cool water of Lake Michigan near Lincoln Park on the city's North Side.

Some 2,400 acres were devastated, up to three hundred people killed.

Damage exceeded two hundred million dollars, an astronomical sum in 1871. The fire took with it some 18,000 structures, including two thousand businesses, forty churches, fifty hotels, thirty banks, half-a-dozen schools, three railway terminals, seven daily newspapers, seven bridges, and hundreds of homes. Two hundred business blocks were wiped out. Thousands of Chicagoans were left homeless.

At the time of the tragedy, Chicago was the nation's fourth most-populous city, behind New York, Philadelphia, and Brooklyn. It was a commercial, transportation, and communications center. So the news went out rapidly of the calamitous setback in Chicago.

Responses and relief supplies came quickly, including from the people in Wisconsin because even other residents of the Badger State were unaware of the catastrophe that had befallen their fellow citizens in Peshtigo.

Chapter 10

October 9, 1871.

The day after.

The ferocious flames had burnt out and given way to an uneasy calm across the devastated region.

For the survivors in Peshtigo and elsewhere, it was a time to try to put the miseries of the previous night behind them and move ahead, however slowly. But many of them could only relive the terror of the three hours that destroyed the town and its surroundings.

When the firewall had moved on, the dead and injured remained in its wake. Hundreds of people huddled in the Peshtigo River. They were at first afraid to leave their watery sanctuary. But many soon noticed that, as the heat of the inferno dwindled, the water had become cold. Even frigid to some. Teeth were chattering and bodies were shaking involuntarily. The river-seekers had experienced one extreme, now another. Others complained of cramps from staying in one place for so long. The cool water only exacerbated their condition. Despite that, many refused to leave their safe haven until they were certain that the danger had passed. They feared another fire could blow in from the same direction as the first. They noticed a breeze blowing at them from the same direction and they were frightened.

By three o'clock on the morning of October 9th, several Peshtigans decided the risk of the continuous cold water was as dangerous as the prospect of a second deadly fire. They left the river, stood dripping at the water's edge, and shivered as the cold night air made their damp clothing most uncomfortable. Then they noticed other ailments: cracked and shriveled skin, swollen throats, lungs filled with remnants of smoke, ash, and other debris, and extreme fatigue. Some remained blinded from the sheer brightness of the flames while others had gone deaf from the roar of the wind and the fire it ushered through their midst.

The physical maladies, however, were inferior to the emotional distress that overwhelmed all of them. They had survived a horrific natural calamity and survived. But they knew some family members and friends had perished. They could not know whether their homes and businesses had been spared.

Now, as they emerged from the water, the lucky ones determined they must walk carefully. Clothing, jewelry, shoes, barrel hoops, horse harnesses and more had been left as the terrified townsfolk hurled themselves into the river. People tripped over these articles and a few folks were burned because they remained overwhelmingly hot, hours after the fire departed.

In the dark, a woman moaned by the riverside. She was scared of water, afraid to enter the river. As the fire bore down, she lay on her stomach near the water. The fire had danced over her, leaving severe burns on her frail body. Two females followed the sound of her cries and reached the woman, who was in excruciating pain. One of them took the damp blanket she had used to cover her own head and dipped it into the cool river. Wringing out the article as much as she could, she returned to the suffering woman, bent down next to her, and began dabbing the dark and blotched skin. The woman screamed but her helper attempted to calm her as she placed the cool blanket on the stricken woman's face, neck, and arms. The Good Samaritan tried to engage the injured woman in conversation, hoping it would distract her from the severe wounds she had received.

"I am Abigail Whitney," she said, her voice trailing off as she uttered her family name. She spoke no more but maintained a low, persistent moan as the pain racked her entire frame. The woman who had come to help continued to offer condolences and encouragement, telling the sufferer she would improve when morning came and medical help arrived. But as she talked to the burn victim, the moaning eventually ceased. Silence. The woman was dead.

With the approaching dawn, there was movement along the water's edge as more Peshtigans left the watery confines which had been their protector for hours. Men and women began milling together to exchange names and discuss strategy. People groped the side of the river for candles, torches, or other sticks which they might use to light the last of the darkness. Some of the wood and much of the metal was still superheated, making it easy to light the implements. Embers still smoldered in places, another source for igniting torches. Eventually, lights flickered on in what had become a growing circle of adults and children. The torches attracted others.

"People," one man said in taking the initiative, "with your permission, let me make several suggestions. We need some younger, able-bodied people to travel to Marinette and to Green Bay. Those folks must report the fire, determine whether those communities suffered, and ask that help be sent. They should go as soon as it is light enough for them to see."

Immediately, several young boys and men stepped forward and offered to make the hikes. Marinette was closer, six miles away. Green Bay was twice as far.

"Tell local authorities we will need food, water, blankets, shelters and whatever else might be useful. And those who go to Green Bay must have the local police contact state agents in Madison. We have a major disaster here and will need help."

Three men decided not to wait. They took a torch and immediately made the trek south toward Green Bay. Two others said they would head to Marinette. They left at first light.

"You will need to swim across the river first," the ad hoc leader advised them. "Our bridge is destroyed."

Later, the young men took their leave and entered the Peshtigo River. They emerged from the river on the other bank, then set off at a jog for their six-mile journey north.

The riverside crowd was expanding in number, as those in the water waded out and those on the eastern shore came across. Still others appeared from different parts of town.

"Now, as to us," the man raised his voice so the growing throng could hear him

"My name is William Sargent and I am a foreman at the Peshtigo Company. I suggest we all huddle together here until the day warms. Later, we can assess the damage to our own homes and to our town. I will ask for volunteers to go out and look for other survivors. As you may have heard, I have asked some young fellas to go off to Green Bay and Marinette to seek help. Let us hope that will come as soon as possible. We will make this our base for now. If there are any serious injuries, bring those people here and people can help one another. I thank God we have been spared, although

Peshtigo seems damaged heavily. So let us remain together here for now, for support and comfort. When it gets lighter, we will decide what to do next. But for now, if Doctor Kelsey can hear me, would you please come to this area. Father Pernin and Reverend Hucklebee, would you also come here. Thank you all and God bless you."

The citizens formed an ever-larger circle. Men extended their arms for their wives and children to cling together for warmth and whatever consolation they could derive from their survival of the most massive firestorm any of them had ever known or experienced. Many shivered in wet clothes and moist coats or blankets. Women and children cried, some men whimpered. Many recited prayers, some in silence, others audibly. Strangers introduced themselves and shared their common pain. Many recounted the events of the previous night. Some were speechless. A few were so drained from the frightful experience they fell asleep. The hours passed slowly but safely.

*   *   *

When the sun peeked over the horizon, it was obscured. Those awake could not be certain whether smoke, dust, or clouds were responsible. Most remained asleep, exhausted from the fire and the fear that went with it.

By eight in the morning, two horse-drawn wagons edged closer to where the survivors' group had congregated. The wagons contained a large tent, which Peshtigo Company officials brought in from an outlying lumber camp, one the fire had missed. Men began immediately to erect the tent, which became a portable hospital for the sick and a haven for the women and children. The men who were not injured began to search both sides of the river for survivors and those wounded. When the tent was completed, men and women worked inside the facility to comfort the ill or injured but all they could offer at this early stage was consolation. There were no medical supplies, no food or drink for the healthy and the infirm. The town had nothing left. It was desolate. Through the morning hours, people discovered that their burning thirst could not be slaked by the Peshtigo River. The presence of hundreds of humans and

Peshtigo

animals and their waste, coupled with carcasses of dead animals and corpses of people, as well as the presence of charred pieces of the bridge and other structures had poisoned the water. It was so toxic that the fish who lived in the river had died and hundreds of their upturned bodies floated along with the current.

A few young men and boys were sent out across the community to find anything edible or potable. They returned to the tent with about a dozen cabbages, scorched on the outside but surprisingly moist and crisp inside. A few women took the vital food and parceled it out to everyone, about a single bite for each survivor.

Several men were dispatched on a reconnaissance tour of the entire town. There were four groups, two traveling to the southwest and southeast with the remaining two fording the river and investigating conditions in the northwest and northeast. As the teams returned and reported their findings, the news was not good.

Two buildings had been found unscathed, one on each side of the river, two structures among the hundreds that had been constructed across Peshtigo. Houses, shops, and barns from one end of town to the other were blackened, reduced to ash. The huge Peshtigo Company mill was largely an ash pile, except for two concrete walls that remained partially intact. Where railroad cars once stood, there were now just four steel wheels. And they showed some signs of melting. The rail lines, nearly completed, were now bent and twisted. The wooden railroad ties had burned away completely.

There were no trees in the center of the community. All had been burned by a fire so hot they disappeared. The ground around the trees was ultra-black. Not only had the flames crawled up the trees but they had burrowed below ground, devouring the roots.

The familiar stores lay in a heap of dust. Some metal and glass objects were found in the rubble but none of it could be put to productive use.

Charred human remains lay sprawled throughout the town. There were many on or near the riverbanks but others were found away from the river, the blaze felling them before they could reach safety. Every animal in the town seemed to be dead. Horses, cows, pigs, dogs, cats, even wild deer and birds were killed in great numbers. Their charred bodies lay everywhere. And beyond the boundaries of Peshtigo, wild and domesticated animals which survived the fire and smoke roamed aimlessly in the fields or forests, desperately seeking food and water. Hundreds of these animals would later die of starvation before rescuers could reach them with supplies.

The Congregational Church was largely destroyed. As the blaze advanced up the spire, the incessant wind pushed hard and the steeple fell to the ground below, with its point lodging in the earth. The rubble that had been the knave of the church sparkled when the sun peeked out from the clouds. Shards of stained glass windows reflected the less-than-bright light. The unfinished Roman Catholic Church met a similar feat.

And amidst the devastation there was at least one miracle. Along the eastern bank of the Peshtigo two men found a newborn, crying and waving its tiny arms. Nearby they found a woman who appeared to have delivered the child during the height of the havoc. The mother was dead. Others told of finding what they thought were three or four infants born overnight but none of them survived the ordeal.

The boys sent off to Marinette completed their task successfully because in early afternoon several wagons filled with bread, water, coffee, and other items arrived. The drivers stopped their teams at the east bank of the river and several volunteers carried the gifts across the water to the tent. The goods were distributed to the sick first, then to women and children, finally to the men and older boys. The ad hoc leaders also determined that, as Doctor J.F. Kelsey had not been found, the wagons would return to Marinette with the most seriously injured or those emotionally distraught for whom evacuation from the death and devastation was a necessity.

While those near the river now had access to food and clean water to drink, it was a different matter for those who lived in the smaller towns or in rural regions. It took up to three days for rescuers to find outlying survivors and minister to their needs.

Father Peter Pernin had joined the ad hoc leaders near the tent the day after the conflagration. He comforted the sick and administered the last rights to the dying. By mid-day he told his associates he wanted to ride one of the wagons back to Marinette. He told the survivors he needed to visit his flock and the Catholic church in Marinette, to attend to their needs. But he promised he would return the next day on another wagon convoy ferrying supplies to the survivors. As he boarded a wagon, Pernin asked the driver about conditions in Marinette.

"No one perished, Father, thank God, but many houses burned."

When the priest asked about the condition of the church, school, and his quarters there, the driver only shook his head.

"All burned," he said after a long pause. The wagon began its trek to Marinette. Father Pernin had more misery to contemplate.

Burial parties were organized and dispatched quickly. They had a monumental task, given the number of bodies near the river. These men and women also knew they had the entire town to cover. Surely the numbers of bodies would run into the hundreds, they feared. The teams consisted of men who dug graves, while the women prepared the bodies for interment. Other men and boys fashioned crosses from charred sections of wood. The cross-beams were tied together by rope, grass, bits of clothing, or whatever the cross makers could scrounge from the desolate landscape.

To the west of the town center, one mercy team made a grim discovery. Lying together were twelve men, women, and children. And a rescuer recognized one of the victims.

"They are all members of one family," he told his colleagues. "It's the Newberry family."

A mass grave was excavated and the victims were laid to rest together, as they had apparently died together. A large cross was pushed into the soil and someone wrote the family name on it with a piece of charred wood. Much later, a proper marker was placed above the burying ground.

It read: "All died October 8, 1871". Then it listed the names of Henry Newberry, 22; Selah F. Newberry, 20; Walter B. Newberry, 12; Louisa, wife of W.B. Newberry, 28; Nellie Newberry, 4; Walter Newberry, 2; Infant Newberry; Edward S. Newberry, 28; Louisa A. Newberry, 19 (Edward's wife); Charles O. Newberry, 32; Franklin H. Newberry, 2; Jessie Newberry, 5.

*   *   *

Maybell Kittner had shepherded her family out of the river water sometime in the middle of the night when the six children and her mother complained of chills in the rapidly-cooling water. She and her sister Nan gathered the others into a tight group and covered them with the damp blankets and other garments which had saved their lives. When the tent arrived and was constructed, Maybell took them all inside. She told the helpers her mother was still tired from the ordeal and the children remained terrorized. Places were made for Mary and her six grandchildren. Nan and Maybell stayed with them for a short time. Then the sisters left their family and went to help others who were in pain or suffering. During a break in their work, Maybell Kittner took Nan aside. She unbuttoned the coat she wore and removed the soiled and damp piece of silk she had managed to save when the wagon had overturned during their escape.

"When life returns to normal, Nan," she said, "I'm going to clean this fabric and make a new Sunday dress. It will be the best and most important dress I shall ever wear. And I will call it the 'fire frock'. No matter where I go or what happens to me, this silk goes with me forever."

*   *   *

A little farther upstream, David Maxon and his children had ducked under the water for hours. When they were standing, they poured water over Maxon's ailing wife, and their mother. When the fire approached, then crossed the river, David ordered his children to stay submerged for as long as they could. If they stayed above water for any length of time, he told them, they would likely be burned. With just seconds to go before the fiery assault, David dropped into the water along with a blanket. He jumped up, covered his wife as she still lay on her partially-submerged bed. Then he sprawled out on top of her, shielding her from the flames, heat, and smoke. The fire darted so rapidly over this part of the river that the Maxon family was spared from certain doom. When the flames passed, though, there was still the lingering smoke and dust to worry about. David Maxon adjured his children not to take deep breaths, as the smoke would harm their lungs. They did as they were told.

Peshtigo

An hour later, with the danger past, he detected the chill in the water and its impact on him. He noticed his youngest children's teeth were chattering, which he concluded was not a good sign.

"Children, we will leave the river now and stop along the bank," he told them.

With twelve-year-old Adam helping, David Maxon managed to drag his ailing wife off the bed and onto the shore. They helped Priscilla lie down, then David and his eldest son returned to the river. Together, they dragged the sodden bed out of the water and set it near Priscilla. With the help of the younger children, they managed to get her back on the bed and covered her with a coat and blanket.

When morning came, David Maxon awakened his children with good news.

"Mother's fever has broken," he told the five children. "And we have survived a most horrible fire. Let us now thank God for sparing us and restoring Mother's health."

They all knelt and prayed.

*   *   *

John Cox had spent four hours in the Peshtigo River, primarily protecting Kate Guillfoyle.

To counteract her gathering anxiety, John had maintained a steady and fearless posture even though his heart beat rapidly and a secret terror raged within him. When he and Kate had made it to the relative safety of the water, the two went toward the middle covering as much of their bodies as possible. When Kate became nervous with the flowing water up to her neck, John held her and spoke soothingly to her. She calmed a bit and he rejoiced secretly that this beautiful young woman was suddenly so dependent on him. Every few minutes he would pull them both under water, to moisten their dried and chapped skin as the massive heat build-up preceded the flames. When their heads were above water, he did all the talking, telling her they would survive the terrible ordeal and that everything would be fine. Then the wave of flames tore through the final row of buildings and down the riverbank.

John had taken Kate into the water just above the Peshtigo Bridge. So when the blaze reached the waterline it leaped onto the wooden span and that kept it away from those in the river nearby. But John had to remain on constant vigil in case some of the wooden beams from the bridge toppled in their direction. In fact, sections of the bridge tipped in all directions. But the hot embers never came close enough to Kate and John to harm them. They were also fortunate because the current took the burning boards and logs downstream, away from their position.

When the Great Fire traversed the river rapidly, it brought flames to both sides of the river. The danger from flames, heat, flying embers, ash, and smoke had enveloped them. They could now feel a sunburn-like heating on their faces and ears so they dropped into the water for several seconds, came back up for just a few seconds to collect their breath, then plunged their heads back under the water. It took nearly an hour of this before the many dangers related to the fire had passed them by. Kate said she was exhausted. John held her close to him and, when the water began to feel cold, he announced that the danger had passed and he would carry her out of the river where they could rest on the bank.

When they reached the river's edge, John Cox set Kate Guillfoyle down on her feet. The two began walking in the dark, feeling their way for a place to settle. They had taken only a few steps when Kate tripped over something and screamed horrifically.

John knelt down in the dark and discovered the body of someone who had never made it to the river refuge. The body was burned so badly John could not tell whether it was male or female, adult or large child.

"It felt so terrible when I touched it," Kate whimpered, and John put an arm around her once more. They walked several more paces until John found a place large enough for them to sit. "Now you lie here," he told her. "Use my blanket as a pillow."

"You must be tired," she replied.

"I am but I will sit up to be sure nothing else comes this way," he said.

She dropped down and lay on her left side, the "pillow" propped under her head. He sat in front of her, poised to react should another fire approach. She grabbed for his hand and clasped it firmly.

"Thank you," she said simply. "You were so strong that I know I would not have survived without you."

Peshtigo

Had she been able to see his face in the dark, she would have detected that he was blushing but also smiling with exultation.

"It was my pleasure," he said. "I am very happy that we made it."

By morning, both were asleep, facing each other, still holding hands. They did not wake up until the tent wagon arrived. John jumped up, volunteering to help set it up. Kate then helped care for the sick. John joined one of the October 9th burial groups. After a while it came to John's own street. There was not a single structure intact, so John Cox was certain that all his possessions were destroyed as well.

John Cox and Kate Guillfoyle were reunited at the end of the day. They had some bread and coffee that had been delivered from Marinette. In fact, John and Kate remained together for days. They had been brought together in tragedy. They had helped each other through the tragedy. They stayed together during the post-fire trauma. They discovered they needed each other now and wanted to be with each other for the future. In the succeeding days, the pair would become much closer.

Three weeks to the day after the Great Peshtigo Fire, John asked Kate to marry him. Without hesitation, she threw her arms around his neck, said "yes", and kissed him.

*   *   *

After a meal and something to drink, the healthy survivors fanned out to look for additional injured survivors, and to bury the dead. As the hours passed, these groups traveled farther from the town center. They journeyed to rural farms and neighboring communities.

Two Peshtigo men came upon the John Church farm several miles west of town, although neither knew the family. From the road, they called out to see whether anyone had survived the holocaust and might need help. They continued calling as they walked down the dirt lane to what looked like the settlement, the house and barn, or at least the remnants of both.

Between two mounds of ash, the rescuers found two badly burned bodies. One was quite a bit larger than the other and there was a tarnished gold wedding band in the dust near the smaller figure. The men concluded it was a man and woman. A bit closer to what they thought must have been the barn, two victims lay on their sides. They were somewhat smaller, so the men concluded they were children. In each case, however, they realized that positive identification was impossible. The men would report back the number of victims they had found and they would ask burying teams to visit the various farms and make graves.

As the two were about to conclude their survey of this devastated property, they chanced upon the grimmest discovery of the day.

Lying on his back was the unburned torso of a young boy. In his right hand he clutched a piece of jagged metal, perhaps a steel band that had surrounded a water bucket. The boy's neck was slashed, the gash extending from his left ear to his Adam's apple. A huge quantity of blood had spilled on the sooty ground. The ash had absorbed some of it, the rest was beginning to dry.

It was twelve-year old Terrence Church. When light had come hours after the fire's visit, he had awakened to find utter desolation in his yard. He noticed the ruins of the farmhouse first, then he saw what he thought were the burned bodies of brothers Ephraim and John Junior. He began to cry but still hoped he might find his mother and father alive. That hope was dashed as he neared the ashes of the barn when he found John and Emma Church lying together, his mother's wedding ring by her side.

Terrence went berserk. He ran across the ravaged yard, begging for help, now that the rest of his family was dead. Then he went back to the place where he had slept. He sat down and wailed uncontrollably for what seemed like hours.

At some point early in the afternoon, Terrence decided he would rather die quickly than to starve to death in this dusty land. He reached for a barrel hoop that rested nearby. It was cool now after the fire but the blaze had caused it to burst, leaving a sharp end.

Without hesitation, Terrence Church dragged the implement across the side of his neck.

The pain was excruciating and he screamed uncontrollably, falling backward. His screams echoed in the treeless terrain. He began to bleed copiously and it took just a few minutes before he

Peshtigo

had lost enough blood for his skin to go pale and his brain to go numb.

Terrence lost consciousness after about twenty minutes. He died shortly thereafter.

*   *   *

It took time but the survivors had calculated a tentative estimate of the dead. They found more than seven hundred bodies in Peshtigo itself. A few hundred more corpses were subsequently reported in outlying farms. A team using a horse and wagon returned from the three Sugar Bush communities with grim news. In Lower Sugar Bush, they had counted one hundred-forty bodies, including every member of twenty families. Moving to Middle Sugar Bush, another fifty corpses lay dead.

And in Upper Sugar Bush they found seventy-seven additional victims. The three small towns lost two hundred-sixty-seven of their citizens, virtually the entire populations.

But there were two small miracles in Upper Sugar Bush.

Terrence Kelly and his son Malachy died when they ran headlong into the fire. Terrence was ultimately identified when recovery teams found the remains of a metal crucifix and chain that he had worn. But wife Penelope and daughter Molly survived by remaining in the pond long after the conflagration had passed, until the water made them cold.

And several hours after the fire, some local volunteers who were scouting the community for bodies stumbled across what at first looked like two more victims. They were children who were not burned although the volunteers assumed they had died of asphyxiation. But when two men attempted to remove the bodies of Aubrey and Charlotte Kelly from beside a garden fence, the sleeping children awoke, dazed and unhurt. They had spent the night sleeping in each other's arms. They were reunited with their mother and sister the next morning.

There may have been a hundred bodies in the town of Oconto. Marinette and Menominee had almost no casualties, although one man who had spent the night on a boat in the Menominee River died after returning to shore. The boat's captain did not know whether the man had fallen victim to a heart attack or from fear or exhaustion. And to the north, where the fire had made its final lunge for life and then burned out in Birch Creek, Michigan, one-fifth of the town's one hundred residents perished. Those twenty-two people were the last victims of the October 8th conflagration.

On the eastern peninsula of the Green Bay, authorities and volunteers found more than two hundred fire victims. They also discovered a wide swathe of destruction. Towns from New Franken to Sturgeon Bay were damaged or wiped out completely.

The survivors knew a final concrete number of the dead was unlikely. Some victims were burned so thoroughly, they disintegrated. Their flesh melted, their bones pulverized to dust. Others may have drowned in the river or nearby streams and ponds, their bodies never found. Still others may have hidden in wells and were incinerated or under buildings and were crushed or burned. Many who were injured and removed from the area later died but their deaths were not recorded properly. And one body, not counted after the fire, was found thirty years after the catastrophe in a swamp near the Peshtigo River in Porterfield. The victim was well preserved, and in fact was petrified.

The estimates put the death toll at some two thousand in Northern Wisconsin and the adjoining part of Michigan. All the deaths occurred within a five-hour period on just one traumatic and tragic night.

*   *   *

As the hundreds of rescuers and care-givers carried out their gruesome tasks, more wagon loads of supplies arrived at the Peshtigo River's edge. Bread, bacon, eggs, carrots, milk, coffee, and water were all dragged to the main tent for storage. Several men had collected unburnt wood and they built a big fire to cook the bacon and heat the carrots and coffee.

At dinnertime, those congregating around the tent were given something substantial to eat and drink. Most sat on the river bank, as they had done during and after the inferno.

As the sun began to set, it was covered by dark clouds. Many were fearful, saying it could be another monster fire about to attack

Peshtigo

them. But no one moved. They had no place to hide and if it were a new fire, the river water was their best, and only, hope for protection.

The clouds grew darker and more ominous and a sense of unease engulfed the crowd. The clouds moved closer to the town.

Then the sky opened and rain fell upon Peshtigo, the first rain in a month.

It was exactly twenty-four hours after the most deadly fire ever to strike North America.

Chapter 11

After the downpour, the weather became sunny again, although cooler than in the days leading up to the firestorm. By the river's edge in Peshtigo, life limped along for the survivors. Some of the injured showed signs of recovery, while others got sicker and died. Scouting parties ventured farther afield to look for the injured and the dead, and to assess the extent of the damage. Wagon-loads of supplies continued arriving from Marinette and Menominee to the north but there had been nothing from the south. Somewhat worryingly, the team sent to Green Bay had not returned yet.

A group of twenty men and five women took on a new task. They had found a small boat which they used to ferry people and supplies across the Peshtigo River and they began constructing a temporary bridge to replace the town span ruined in the fire. They took much of the debris from in or near the river and began piling it in the riverbed at its most shallow section near the center of town. On top of that they planned to haul some relatively flat planks which would allow people to walk across gingerly without getting wet. They were putting plenty of wood, metal and dirt into the river and they guessed, and hoped, it would hold the planks. The town could not afford another tragedy, with people, horses, and wagons toppling into the river from an unsafe bridge and drowning. So they went slowly and methodically to get it right. They even discussed allowing only foot-traffic on the span.

In the afternoon Father Peter Pernin returned to Peshtigo from Marinette. He was greeted warmly by those in and near the huge tent, which had now become the heartbeat of the town. The priest went first to visit the most seriously ill. He gave the last rites of the Roman Catholic Church to several people who suffered severe burns and who were losing their struggle to survive. Then he visited others, less sick, who were lounging near the tent or who had made their home temporarily on the riverbank.

As he once more scanned what was left of the town, he was amazed at the desolation. Houses, barns, shops, trees, fences that had stood so securely just three days ago were now ash and dust. He decided to walk a few blocks but found the going difficult and the view depressing. With every step, his black shoes sank in the deep ash. While he saw no human bodies, as they had been collected and buried, dead and decaying animals littered the streets, creating a highly unpleasant odor.

He ventured toward the site of his new church, although it was hard to pinpoint its exact location because every building was gone. Eventually he found the remnants of the steeple, half intact, the rest melted. His small rectory was destroyed as well. Father Pernin dropped to his knees in the thick ashes. He made the Sign of the Cross and prayed, thankful for his own salvation and resigned that the will of God had taken both his houses of worship, here and in Marinette. Still, despite his deep and abiding faith, he began to weep at the sight of the devastation. Then he rose and looked for the burial site of his religious treasures. He came upon the spade of his shovel. The wooden handle had been burned away but the metal was still intact. When he reached the place where he thought the underground repository might be, he began unearthing the dust. After the first foot of digging, he knew he was off target. So he moved a bit to his left but still nothing. He went in the other direction and then the metal spade struck other objects. Now he dug with his bare hands to uncover the church articles. But to his great chagrin, all of the objects were destroyed. The fire had burned down into the ground as well as up into the sky, so sacred things below the surface were doomed.

He made another grim series of discoveries next. His dog's bones lay in a sandy pile not far from his house and the remains of his horse were at the edge of the church property. Father Pernin could only speculate that when he released the horse to find its own safety, the animal must have returned to familiar territory and to its death. Father Pernin knew it was time to leave this area.

As he returned to the tent area, a man ran up to him, breathless.

"Father, I am so glad I found you," he blurted out. "It is a great miracle,"

The man took the priest's arm and dragged him toward the river, then to the place where Father Pernin had pulled his wagon containing the church tabernacle. The two men saw that everything in the area was charred by the fire. But in the middle of the detritus the tabernacle bobbed in the river water, still intact and still white in a sea of black objects.

The men waded into the river immediately, pushed some of the wooden debris away, and retrieved the sacred receptacle of the Blessed Sacrament. When they reached the shore, the priest asked the man to join him in a prayer of thanksgiving.

*   *   *

The fellowship and cooperation of the survivors had reached remarkable levels in the two days since the great conflagration. Citizens had comforted friends and assisted strangers in their shared dismay.

But in the late afternoon, the tone of the crowd changed. The comradery was shattered. Two men from the ad hoc security force dragged another man toward the tent. They took the man before the acknowledged leaders of the new community.

"We caught him stealing from the bodies of the victims," one of the lawmen said.

The leaders organized a jury, listened to the story of the security men, then asked the defendant to explain himself. He offered no defense of his actions, other than to say he had been left with nothing and had to try to find things to re-start his shattered life.

The jury's punishment was swift. The declared him guilty and sentenced the man to death by hanging, immediately. Someone found an iron chain, used in normal times to draw and drag logs from the river into the Peshtigo Company mill. The chain was wrapped around the man's neck and two men on either side of the defendant began to pull it toward them, tightening the neck loop.

The man screamed for mercy incessantly, even as the noose grew tighter.

At last, the jury foreman ordered the men to stop pulling the iron chain. He ordered the man to his knees, instructing him to beg for the pardon of the jury. The frightened burglar did so and the jury let him go. The condemned man thanked them, got to his feet, and ran toward the river. He swam across and then continued running east.

Peshtigo

*   *   *

By mid-day on Tuesday, October 10th, the Peshtigo party dispatched to Green Bay arrived in the large city. The men ran immediately to the local police station. They spoke first to two officers, who summoned the police chief. The scouts recounted their horrific story a second time. The Chief-of-Police wasted no time. He escorted the men to the Post and Telegraph Office, just a block away. The police official instructed the telegrapher on duty to send an urgent message to the state capital, Madison, addressed to Governor Lucius Fairchild. It was transmitted within fifteen minutes.

The police chief then took the Peshtigans to City Hall, where he introduced them to the Mayor. Now they related the fiery events a fourth time, ending by explaining that the survivors had no food or shelter or even a change of clothes. As the Mayor was deciding how to respond, an aide brought another man into his office. Captain Thomas Howley had arrived at Green Bay's port aboard his steamer The Union from the town of Menominee.

"Your honor," Howley began. "I have the fearful and heart-sickening news that the village of Peshtigo was entirely destroyed by fire on Sunday evening and that the village of Menekaune was swept away."

Now the Mayor and Chief-of-Police of Green Bay had heard of the tragedy twice within a very few minutes. The two officials conferred briefly, then the Mayor called in his assistants and ordered an immediate effort to send food, clothes, and more tents to Peshtigo by land. Similar but smaller relief supplies were to be gathered and put about Captain Howley's ship to be taken to the survivors in Menekaune.

As the relief effort began in Green Bay, the telegram was delivered to the Governor's Mansion in Madison. It was the first word of the tragedy to reach the capital. But Lucius Fairchild was out of town.

Ironically, he had organized a relief train to take supplies to victims of the Chicago fire, which he had learned about just yesterday. The governor, many of his aides, and most members of the Wisconsin legislature had boarded the train for Chicago. They would help distribute supplies and assist with clearing away debris and erecting temporary shelters for the homeless and dispossessed.

Governor Fairchild's wife had elected to stay home. He needed her in Madison in case any problems developed. He advised her where the Wisconsin delegation would be staying during their mercy mission to Chicago, should she need to contact him. But when he took this precaution, Fairchild thought of potential problems that were political or parochial in nature, never cataclysmic.

Mrs. Fairchild was writing letters in the Mansion's solarium. A butler entered the room and handed her the telegram, advising her it was deemed urgent. He departed and, now alone, she read the message sent from Green Bay.

"Good God," she cried aloud to no one. "This is appalling."

She left her unfinished letters and dashed to the wing of the Governor's House where his office was situated. An aide was working in the anteroom. Mrs. Fairchild handed the telegram to him. He gasped midway through it.

"We must contact Mister Fairchild immediately," she told the aide. "He must return here at once to deal with our own tragedy. I will begin coordinating relief efforts immediately from Madison. But we must get temporary housing, food, water, and clothing up to Peshtigo as quickly as possible."

The Governor's assistant said he would race to the telegraph office in the State Capitol to send an urgent message to Governor Fairchild. He suggested that Mrs. Fairchild go to the Capitol as well and talk to staffers in the Executive and Legislative branches about the most expeditious way to gather supplies and ship them north. He added that the Wisconsin militia might have the most supplies available for rapid distribution.

"You must also contact the local newspapers," the Governor's wife told the man. "We must get the word out beyond Wisconsin. We must ask for donations of money and supplies for the poor victims of the tragic fire."

The two prepared to depart the Governor's Mansion to begin their life-saving tasks.

Urgent messages were sent to Chicago, to Governor Fairchild, and to the leaders of the state legislature. They were apprised of the

Peshtigo

holocaust that had befallen Northern Wisconsin, advised that Mrs. Fairchild was spearheading a relief undertaking in Madison, and asked to return to the capital city as soon as possible. The telegram also suggested the Governor ask officials of Chicago and Illinois to return the favor, by helping the victims in Peshtigo and vicinity.

The aide, whose name was Barnaby Jackson, next sent a telegram to the editors of the local newspapers. He asked them to contact people in Green Bay for details, to print news of the great fire, and to implore readers to contribute to the growing relief effort. Jackson also exhorted the editors to send word to papers in Milwaukee, Chicago, Detroit, and beyond about the conflagration that had destroyed Northern Wisconsin and neighboring Michigan.

Wisconsin's First Lady wasted no time. She contacted state and military officials, as well as the higher-ups of the railroad, wagon builders, food stores, clothiers, blanket makers, and the company in Milwaukee which made tents. In each case she explained the tragedy and the urgent needs of the survivors. She urged each to coordinate efforts through the Governor's office but to gather relief goods speedily and get them to Peshtigo by rail and road as quickly as possible. And she asked them to contact others to help out.

She went to the University of Wisconsin and the city's largest hospital, begging doctors and nurses to rush to the north woods temporarily to care for the physical and emotional needs of the victims. Mrs. Fairchild asked the telegraph company to work rapidly to restore communications with the towns now cut off after the fire's wrath.

She contacted banks, seeking monetary donations for the short term, and records' searches so the residents of northern communities would have access to their savings as bank records were likely destroyed by the blaze.

Within hours, there was movement on many fronts. Within days, a steady stream of goods and services was pouring into Peshtigo.

Tents were erected throughout the community. Ad hoc grocery stores were set up on each side of the river. Clothes, shoes, coats and blankets were distributed from a large tent erected near the temporary Peshtigo bridge. Wagons carried the ill from the tent to a hospital in Green Bay.

Hotels there became hospital annexes, housing the wounded until they recovered. These temporary facilities were manned by doctors and nurses from Milwaukee and Madison. Other medical professionals donated their time and talent in Peshtigo, Oconto, Marinette, and in the eastern peninsula at New Franken and Sturgeon Bay. As it had not been affected by the flames, there were hotels and homes in Sturgeon Bay that were converted to medical facilities quickly and efficiently.

Sixty children who had survived, only to discover their parents had perished, were taken to a newly-built tent barracks behind the Presbyterian Church in Marinette. The facility was operated by parishioners, with the help of some nurses from Green Bay and a physician from Racine, in the southern part of the state.

The United States Army sent two-hundred-thousand rations of hard bread, bacon, and beans to both sides of the Green Bay. It also sent blankets, boots, and some clothing for adults.

Water became perhaps the most desperately-sought commodity. Because so many humans, animals, and fish had fallen into and fouled the Peshtigo River, many of whom died, the water from the river was unfit to drink. It carried a taste of toxic lye for weeks following the fire.

Governor Fairchild, back in his state capital, augmented the efforts of his tireless wife. He sought monetary donations from public and private sources, both inside Wisconsin and beyond its boundaries. And he sent state engineers and other public employees to assess the damage and report on the long-term needs of the ruined communities in the northeastern corner of the state. Within days, the Governor reported that $141,568.49 had come in, mainly from private sources across Wisconsin. As time passed, pledges of support came from other states whose residents had been horrified by newspaper details of the October 8th inferno. Readers in New York, Washington and other cities could not imagine such a catastrophe.

Nonetheless, despite the mammoth salvage efforts, many who had survived the terrible ordeal of the fire died of starvation before food and water could reach them in more rural areas.

Federal government officials rushed to the region as well, to assist Wisconsin state employees in dealing with the aftermath.

Peshtigo

They concluded there were several fires, perhaps scores of them, which rampaged across Northern Wisconsin and Upper Michigan from about seven o'clock that Sunday evening until about two the next morning. The blazes on the western side of the Green Bay charred an area sixty miles long and more than fifteen miles wide. On the east side of the Bay, the path of destruction was narrower: fifty miles long, five miles across.

The greatest damage on the western side was to Peshtigo. But there was widespread destruction as well in Oconto, the Sugar Bush communities, and Menekaune in Wisconsin and Birch Creek, Michigan.

On the eastern peninsula, New Franken was hit hard, as was Williamsonville, Brussels, Lincoln, Forestville, Kewaunee, Pierce, Casco, Carlton, and Ahnapee.

A relief worker who had traveled from Boston estimated some four thousand people were left destitute by the series of fires. The Governor's office placed the figure between three- and four-thousand.

As if the fires and their aftermath were not enough, an outbreak of smallpox surfaced in Peshtigo soon after the flames died out. Additional medical personnel were rushed into town to deal with the disease. Workers constructed an isolation facility to house those who contracted the illness. One doctor concluded the smallpox had developed from germs carried in the clothing and bedding of the survivors.

When the immediate needs were fulfilled, residents and businessmen began toting up their financial losses. The largest employer, the Peshtigo Company, determined the destruction of its facilities and the products contained therein was worth more than one million dollars, an astronomical figure.

Many families lost all they had.

But the town of Peshtigo vowed to rebuild itself from the destruction. And from the ashes, there was remarkable, phoenix-like progress.

The North Western Railroad re-constructed its destroyed track lines in just two months from Fort Howard to Peshtigo.

Vast stretches of fire-cleared land created thousands of new acres of tillable land for agriculture. People snapped up the property and set up new farms.

Homes were constructed quickly. Some Peshtigans even joked that houses were being built like wildfire. Shops were rebuilt. Banks reopened and many depositors received their money lost in the Great Peshtigo Fire.

Logging operations resumed, although shanty boys now had to venture farther from town to harvest the seas of trees.

Within three years of the cataclysm, Peshtigo was once again whole. Vestiges of the fire were nearly gone. The town got its own newspaper. The *Peshtigo Times* would serve *"The City Reborn From The Ashes Of America's Most Disastrous Fire"*, which it printed on its masthead.

Survivors would swap stories for years, of terror and destruction, of destitution and rehabilitation. But one story emerged that was particularly poignant for the people of Northern Wisconsin.

Christian Felch had finally become successful at homesteading. He had settled a twenty-acre parcel near the Menominee River, north of Peshtigo. It was his third such attempt. The German immigrant, still learning to speak English, had cleared much of his land, constructed a log cabin, a root-house, a well, and a work shed. His first crops of onions, potatoes, and pumpkins were struggling to survive because of the prolonged dry spell of 1871.

On the night of October 8th, Christian Felch and his wife Josephine, who was seven months pregnant, were in their cabin. She was baking bread, he was reading the Bible. The noise of horses jolted Chris from his rocking chair. Two riders stopped when he opened the cabin's front door.

"A forest fire is coming," the pair of riders shouted in unison, "and coming fast," one of them added. They galloped off away from the approaching conflagration.

Christian ordered his wife to gather the children, from Josephine's marriage to Charles Meyer who had died the year before, and to run toward a neighboring farm some two miles away.

As they ran off, Christian gathered his valuables and paper records. He found his shovel and buried the possessions under the root-cellar, about a foot below ground. He marked the spot with two large stones, then raced off to catch his family.

When Chris Felch reached the Bernardy farm, he found his own wife and children along with members of the Rawn and Hattenberg families. But the Bernardy clan was not there. They had run for the Menominee River and safety. It was too late for the other families to reach the river, so they elected to lie on the ground near the Bernardy barn, putting their heads into the dirt.

They lay there for hours, reciting prayers, as the warmth of the fire and its accompanying thick smoke came toward them. But by the time it had reached the area near Menominee, the great fire had lost its strength. The flames faded. All three families were unhurt, although they suffered from smoke inhalation which led to long bouts of choking and coughing.

After an early-morning meal of bread and water, the three families said prayers of thanksgiving for their deliverance from a fiery death, then each family returned home.

Christian Felch was shocked to discover that only his root-cellar somehow remained standing. The papers and other treasures were tarnished and singed but they had survived. But his cabin and shed were nothing but smoldering embers. The kitchen stove still stood but its metal was melted and twisted out of shape. Christian went to the oven and with the aid of a stick, he pried open the oven door. Inside, untouched, was a loaf of bread. Blackened.

The outside of the bread was like charcoal but the inside was edible. It was the only food the Felch family had the day after the blaze. Christian would later find other items of food and drink until relief help arrived.

A Red Cross worker named Rose David Armour invited Josephine and the children to live with her until the family could find another home or a replacement log cabin.

It was mid-October but Chris promised his wife a new cabin by Christmas. For the next few weeks, he did all that he could to secure the needed building materials. He was ready to begin construction but the local mill had not been able to provide the necessary lumber, despite repeated requests from Chris Felch. The mill owners reiterated their dilemma: so much lumber was needed to reconstruct the homes and businesses in Northern Wisconsin that people had to wait their turn.

He despaired that he would be unable to keep his promise to Josephine.

But on December 24th a local lumber camp crew came to his property. They brought wood and their own manpower. The lumber team helped Christian Felch build a two-story wooden cottage in one day. At the end of the day, the proud new homeowner offered the lumber men drinks of beer and he offered them best wishes for the happy Christmas.

The next morning, Chris moved in the family furniture. He had also chopped a small pine tree in the woods near his new home. Then he drove his wagon to Rose Armour's house and collected his family. By mid-day, they were settled in their new home.

The Felch family decorated their tree with berries. They celebrated Christmas in front of the tree, with a fire blazing in the new fireplace, while a ham, potatoes, and bread cooked in a brand new oven.

It was the best Christmas Christian Felch could ever remember.

www.ingramcontent.com/pod-product-compliance
Lightning Source LLC
Chambersburg PA
CBHW070640050426
42451CB00008B/238